Dear Lord,

They Want

ME

to Give the

DEVOTION

Again

John D. Schroeder & Shane M. Groth

Dear Lord,

They Want

ME

to Give the

DEVOTION

Again

DIMENSIONS

FOR LIVING

NASHVILLE

DEAR LORD, THEY WANT ME TO GIVE THE DEVOTION AGAIN
Copyright © 2001 by Dimensions for Living

This book is printed on elemental-chlorine–free paper.

Library of Congress Cataloging-in-Publication Data

Schroeder, John D.
    Dear Lord, they want me to give the devotion, again! / John D. Schroeder & Shane M. Groth.
    p. cm.
    ISBN 0-687-09820-3 (alk. paper)

    1. Devotional literature, English.   I. Groth, Shane M.   II. Title.
    BV4801 .S285 2001
    242—dc21

                                      00-052329

01 02 03 04 05 06 07 08 09 10—10 9 8 7 6 5 4 3 2

MANUFACTURED IN THE UNITED STATES OF AMERICA

Contents

―――――――――――― ◑◐◑ ――――――――――――

Introduction

After the release of our first devotional, *Dear Lord, They Want Me to Give the Devotions!* readers often told us about using the book to give a devotion and how they personalized the topic to make the story their own. When it came to doing a sequel, we decided to focus on that aspect of sharing your faith; and that is how this book was born.

This second devotional is intended to move readers from leading a devotion to sharing their faith in a personal and nonthreatening way.

How to Use This Book

The format is the same as our first book. Each of the fifty devotions is listed alphabetically by topic. For example, if you are half way through a campaign to raise money for your church, you might want to use the devotion on "Accomplishment" (p. 17). If crime is an issue in your community, you might select the devotion on that topic. Look through the topics to find the one that meets your needs and interests. The devotional topics are listed in the contents.

You can also use this book for personal devotions or weekly meetings. You can start from the beginning and use one devotion per week. The fifty devotions can cover a year of meetings.

The Purpose of a Devotion

What is a devotion? Often the fear of leading a devotion comes from not understanding the true purpose of a devotion. The purpose of a devotion is to:

• Show how your faith has been helpful for you.
• Connect the Bible with daily life.
• Build rapport with others (group building).
• Celebrate how God has acted in your life.
• Raise an issue or faith concern that needs to be addressed.
• Build up the community of faith with a word of encouragement.

What is a devotion not? You'll notice that sharing theological expertise is *not* the purpose of a devotion. You need not have an advanced degree in theology or be a pastor to share a meaningful devotion. A devotion from the heart—sharing what is personally important to you at the time—is much more appreciated and uplifting than a brief Bible study. The main purpose of a devotion is to share how God has been part of the struggles and joys you experience in your daily walk of faith.

How to Personalize Devotions

This book of devotions differs from our first book. Each devotion is followed by three ways to modify the reading to include personal beliefs and stories. Again, the devotions can be read just as they are for personal or group use. If you wish, however, you can deliver a personal devotion by adding your own experiences and views to the existing text.

Sharing your faith with others through the use of a devotion is not as scary as it may seem. It can be a very natural part of your reading to include your own views and experiences. Chances are you selected a specific topic in this book because the topic is of interest to you. Personalization is taking the process one step further and talking about your interest.

The three ideas for modification that follow each devotion in this book are a starting point. One of the ideas for modification is to tell why you selected this topic in the first place. Talk about what your experience has been and why the topic is important to you. This can be as simple as making a few notes on an index card and reading your notes at the conclusion of the devotion. You could also say why you selected this topic before you begin reading the devotion. Again, your brief personal comments can greatly enhance the devotional experience for your audience.

There are other ideas given on how to make a devotion your own. You might want to share how the topic relates to your life. Perhaps you have an experience to share with the group. If you don't have an experience, you might have an observation about the topic that was not covered by the author. You can also expand on the views of the author as given in the devotion. And you can even disagree with the writer's point of view! The point is to share your feelings and your own story in a manner that is comfortable for you.

Sharing experiences of faith is nothing new. Look at the Bible itself. The Bible is a collection of stories and experiences of God's people. It is a reflection of human life and how God loved, nurtured, and interacted with his creation. The faults and strengths of the human race are told through the stories of the Bible. You read about the real experiences of real people. The Bible reveals what people thought, what they experienced, and how they acted or reacted in any given situation. Like the stories of the Bible, your devotion can be a glimpse at an experience you had and how it relates to your faith in God.

You'll note that each devotion has three basic parts: (1) an opening Bible verse related to the topic; (2) a story, anecdote, or example that pertains to the topic and Bible verse; and (3) ways the Scripture verse relates, challenges, or encourages us in our lives of faith today. For more on the three basic parts of a devotion, see the section "Creating Your Own Devotion from Scratch."

Personalizing the devotion is as simple as substituting any or all of these three basic components. For example, suppose your group wants to start a new program. You decide that the devotion on "Action" is appropriate. To personalize the devotion you could (1) discuss a Bible verse that reflects the theme—keeping the rest of the devotion as is; (2) add an example from your own life where an obstacle was overcome with God's help; or (3) make your own connection about how faith and trust in God has worked miracles in the past in your life. Any or all of these three components could be added to make the devotion more personal.

Again, once you select the topic, the choices are up to you. You might use one or more of the ideas for modification to make the story your own. Your thoughts and experiences can help your audience relate to you and your topic. Personalization brings the topic alive.

Finally, share your thoughts and experiences as your comfort level dictates. If this is your first time, a few brief personal comments at the end of the devotion might be the right touch. If you are more ambitious, say what is in your heart. Be honest and natural. Your audience will appreciate your openness and support you in taking a risk to reveal your feelings or experiences. By sharing something personal, you are "making the gospel story your own."

You could also add a prayer at the end of the devotion for inspiration or encouragement. See the section "How to Pray in Public."

Creating Your Own Devotion from Scratch

The ultimate in personalization is to create your own devotion from scratch. You can do this by simply using the same three components previously discussed. Keep in mind that if something is interesting or important for you, it will likely be important for others. Here are the three basic steps.

First: Faith motivator. If possible, begin with a Bible verse that has been on your mind recently. What issues has it raised? Why has the verse been important for you? How has the verse connected with your daily life? What themes has it addressed?

Second: Faith story. Think of a story, anecdote, or example from your own life that you feel connects to the topic and to the Bible verse. What experience comes to mind when you think of the topic or Bible verse you selected? Don't sweat over finding the exciting or unique experience— usually the common experiences work best as people can easily relate to them.

Third: Faith in action. This is the time to show how your story relates, challenges, or encourages people in their lives of faith today. How was God working or speaking to you in that particular situation?

Keep in mind that devotions need not be prepared at the last minute. Keep your eyes and ears open for examples, situations, or Scripture that is meaningful to you. Write these down when they happen. Jot down poems that speak to you. Write down how the Spirit has spoken to you during a time of prayer. Save these in your folder for future reference.

How to Pray in Public

You may want to end your devotion with a short prayer. Praying in public is similar to giving a devotion—we pray to share how God is active in our lives today. Prayer in its simplest form is talking with God. It is not an occasion to impress others with how religious we are or to show how much we know about the Bible. Nor is prayer a platform to show how eloquently we speak. Prayer in its best form is an expression to God of our feelings, using the words that come to us at the time. (If you do not feel comfortable praying spontaneously, write down your prayer beforehand and simply read it out loud.)

With this in mind—that the best prayer is a prayer from the heart—here are a few suggestions to quickly prepare for praying out loud:

1. Think of the occasion. Is the group gathering for a Bible study? A funeral? A meal?

2. Are there any special requests for those gathered together? Is there an important observation or acknowledgment that should be made?
3. Be honest with your feelings. Let your words reflect your joy, your sadness, or your worry. At a loss for words? People can relate to that.
4. Be thankful. On all occasions we can give thanks to God.
5. Be brief. Keep your prayer short. People will appreciate your conservation of words.

Using Follow-up Questions

Once you have presented your devotion on the topic of your choice, you may want to continue the discussion of the topic by using one or more follow-up questions. Using questions to start a discussion after your devotion can be valuable in gaining a deeper understanding of issues and feelings related to the topic. Here are some tips:

1. Questions should be nonthreatening and serve the purpose of starting a dialogue. Avoid questions that simply repeat information from the text or questions that can be answered with a yes or no answer.
2. Focus questions on your particular group or issue. Focus on how something challenges or encourages.
3. Set a time limit for the discussion and tell your group how much time you want to devote to discussion.
4. If you ask a question and no one responds, give your own thoughts and feelings on the subject. Serve as an example that it is safe to express an opinion.
5. If time permits, ask for other questions on the topic from those in your group.
6. Remember to thank everyone for participating in the discussion.

Accomplishment

So shall my word be that goes out of my mouth; it shall not return to me empty, but it shall accomplish that which I propose, and succeed in the thing for which I sent it.

(Isaiah 55:11)

The story is told of a man who was shoveling his driveway on a cold winter day. Mother Nature had just deposited ten inches of heavy snow. A boy came by and asked the man if he could shovel the driveway for him. It seemed like an odd request because the job was partially complete. He asked the boy why he was offering his services. The boy replied that he got most of his work from people who were half done.

It has been said that the world is full of people with good intentions. We often begin an ambitious project with zeal. It can be quite easy to start a task. We can begin reading a book, begin attending a class, or begin a cleaning project; and that is as far as we get. We get distracted. Something more interesting comes along. We run out of energy. Often the result is that our best intentions get us off to a good start and nothing more.

This devotion could end right here. Instead, the writer continues sentence by sentence. He has a goal in mind. That is how all projects begin, with an idea or goal. It is then up to us to take the journey from concept to completion. That is how things progress, one step at a time, one step after another. Our eyes need to be focused on accomplishment.

Just as we want to finish what we start, God also wants us to reach our goals. Many people do go the distance. They may not be as smart as we are; they may not possess great talent; they may not even have the proper skills; but they have one thing that so many people lack: they don't have sense enough to quit. Regardless of how much time it takes, they finish the job.

What does God want us to accomplish? He has asked us to make disciples of all nations, to feed the hungry, to help the poor, to visit those in prison, and to be his arms and legs. Our unfinished tasks cannot further God's kingdom. We have been given the brains to overcome the obstacles in front of us. As Christians we are to encourage one another and to lend a hand when we can. This help and encouragement from others is how God empowers us toward accomplishment.

Do you have something you want to accomplish? Take up the challenge. Satisfy your own conscience and sense of responsibility. Go where God directs you. And let God be your partner as you finish what you start!

To make this devotion your own:

• Share why you selected this devotion to read.
• Use this devotion as a lead-in to talking about an unfinished church project.
• Share a dream or goal you wish to accomplish.

Action

Faith by itself, if it is not accompanied by action, is dead.
(James 2:17 NIV)

Actress Helen Hayes tells about the time she found herself in the midst of a dogfight. She learned an important lesson from the experience.

I was wheeling a baby carriage, my pet cocker spaniel trotting beside me. Without warning, three dogs—an Afghan, a Saint Bernard and a Dalmatian—pounced on the cocker and started tearing him to pieces. I shrieked for help. Two men in a car stopped, looked, and drove on. When I saw that I was so infuriated that I waded in and stopped the fight myself. My theatrical training never stood me in better stead. My shouts were so authoritative, my gestures so arresting, I commanded the situation like a lion-tamer and the dogs finally slunk away.

Looking back, I think I acted less in anger than from a realization that I was on my own, that if anybody was going to help me at the moment, it had to be myself. *(This I Believe,* ed. Edward P. Morgan [New York: Simon & Schuster, 1952], p. 65)

Although you may have never found yourself in the midst of a dogfight, chances are you can remember a time when you discovered it was up to you to take immediate action in a crisis. God calls us to action many times during life, but it is up to us whether and how we respond.

Like Helen Hayes, we can use our life experiences and skills to solve a situation. You'll often find that God not only provides the tools to face a challenge but also gives us challenges to help us learn and grow. God wants us to take action in a world that often needs our help.

So the next time you are faced with a challenge, look to God for strength and take action. Your words and deeds can change lives.

As Theodore Roosevelt once said, "Do what you can, with what you have, where you are." That is all God asks, and it's also a formula for meeting any crisis.

To make this devotion your own:

• Share some thoughts on how you prepare for challenges in life.
• Discuss a crisis you faced and how God helped you.
• Tell why you selected this devotion to share.

Angels

After the sabbath, as the first day of the week was dawning, Mary Magdalene and the other Mary went to see the tomb. And suddenly there was a great earthquake; for an angel of the LORD, descending from heaven, came and rolled back the stone and sat on it. His appearance was like lightning, and his clothing white as snow. For fear of him the guards shook and became like dead men. But the angel said to the women, "Do not be afraid; I know that you are looking for Jesus who was crucified. He is not here; for he has been raised, as he said. Come, see the place where he lay. Then go quickly and tell his disciples, 'He has been raised from the dead, and indeed he is going ahead of you to Galilee; there you will see him.' This is my message for you."

(Matthew 28:1-7)

Angels have been quite in vogue the last few years. They've popped up in movies, on television programs, in artwork, in books by the score, and even on wallpaper. Angels continue to be a popular topic, perhaps because they touch a yearning within each of us. We want God to be present in our lives. We want to believe that God gets involved in our lives, even if it happens through an angel.

The danger, however, can be to get so caught up in the sensational stories of these heavenly beings that we miss God. We get so excited about the angel rolling away the stone from the tomb that we forget about Christ, the Resurrected One. Angels exist, but they are only pointers to a greater truth—that God exists in our life and in our world through the power of the Resurrection. Death may surround us, yes, but it is life in the midst of death that God gives to each of us.

The message of the angel on Easter morning is that God is with us, in our midst, even though we may not recognize God's presence. God is with us, comforting us, in the midst of our fear and doubt. Like Mary mistaking the risen Christ for the gardener, we may miss or mistake God's very presence, but it doesn't make God any less real. God is present; God is with us, more in the ordinary than in the sensational. God came to be with us, to surround us, each and every moment of our day.

The message of the angel on Easter was to let Jesus' disciples know that the same Jesus who had walked the earth, who had mingled with them, who had experienced the surprise of the sunrise and the disappointment of relationships, had died and risen for them. The angel was there to remind them that in the midst of the ordinary an extraordinary God came to be with them, to love them and to save them.

If you want to see angels, look at the lives of your family, your friends, your loved ones, your coworkers and those in your church. For there you will find the resurrected Christ working his extraordinary love in ordinary ways.

To make this devotion your own:

• Talk about a person in your own life who you think is an "angel."
• Relate a story where you believe an angel was present in your life or someone else's life.
• What things or events in your own life, other than angels, have pointed you to God?

Ask

Jesus answered them, "Have faith in God. Truly I tell you, if you say to this mountain, 'Be taken up and thrown into the sea,' and if you do not doubt in your heart, but believe that what you say will come to pass, it will be done for you. So I tell you, whatever you ask for in prayer, believe that you have received it, and it will be yours."

(Mark 11:22-24)

It was getting close to Christmas. Two weeks left and there was still shopping to do for the kids. Michael, the six-year-old, wanted a Lego® set. Specifically he wanted one of those big Lego sets with the pirates and the ship and the island and the parrot and the treasure and the palm trees and the—well, you get the picture. It was a big set. Michael had been looking at this set from a page in an old magazine that he kept either under his bed or under his pillow, depending on the day. He sat mesmerized as he imagined playing with all the different pieces.

The parents figured the set would be easy enough to find once they actually started looking for it. So they stopped at all the local toy stores with the model number in hand only to find that the set had been discontinued several months earlier. It was no longer available. For some reason the toy company had stopped making that set.

The parents broke the news to Michael as best they could, thinking he would be disappointed. But he wasn't. They told him again the next night just to make sure he had gotten the message—there would be no pirate Lego set for Christmas. "That's OK," he answered, as if to reassure them. "I prayed to God last night and asked him to somehow get the set for me. You don't have to worry about it."

"Michael, you don't understand," they repeated. "Nobody has the set. They don't even make it anymore. It's been discontinued for six to twelve months. We've looked everywhere for it, and nobody has it. I'm not even sure God can get it for you." And then, thinking about Michael's fragile faith, they added something about the reality of prayer and what kind of prayer God answers.

A few days before Christmas the mother stopped by yet another toy store. Though the situation seemed way beyond hope, she looked in the Lego® section to see what they had. On the bottom shelf, covered with dust and lots of other toys, was a pirate ship—the discontinued set Michael wanted.

Michael got his pirate set for Christmas, and the parents received a valuable lesson in prayer. Michael had asked God for something very important to him. He had believed and never doubted for a moment, even though the two most important people in his life—his parents—had tried to talk him out of it. He had asked. He believed. And he received.

Faith is so simple through the eyes of a child. It is so real. It is so easy. Why wouldn't God give God's children the things they need and ask for? We need to spend more time behind such childlike eyes. We need to be quicker to ask God for those things we need. For "whatever you ask for in prayer, believe that you have received it, and it will be yours" (Mark 11:24).

To make this devotion your own:

- Share whether you ask God for things or tend to keep silent.
- Recall a time God answered a prayer in your life.
- Reflect on what Jesus meant when he said, *"Whatever* you ask for in prayer . . . "* What does Jesus mean by "whatever"?

Bloodhounds

Finally, beloved, whatever is true, whatever is honorable, whatever is just, whatever is pure, whatever is pleasing, whatever is commendable, if there is any excellence and if there is anything worthy of praise, think about these things. Keep on doing the things that you have learned and received and heard and seen in me, and the God of peace will be with you.
(Philippians 4:8-9)

Bloodhounds are known for their amazing sense of smell. One bloodhound in particular, Nick Carter, has helped put six hundred criminals behind bars with the help of his snout. Bloodhounds can pick up scents and smells that are days old and track them for one hundred miles. In fact, the nose of the bloodhound is so well respected that the evidence they sniff out is often admissible in court.

While we will never have the nose of a bloodhound, we can train ourselves to sniff out the good that is in the world. We can focus on the positive, the God-inspired, the Spirit-led. We can be diligent about looking for the best that is in the world. The apostle Paul puts it this way: "Finally, beloved, whatever is true, whatever is honorable, whatever is just, whatever is pure, whatever is pleasing, whatever is commendable, if there is any excellence and if there is anything worthy of praise, think about these things."

The apostle Paul encourages us not only to notice everything that is good, but to be diligent about seeking out that which is right and true and honorable. We are to be bloodhounds with a purpose. We are to be bloodhounds with a nose that detects anything good. Finding the good helps us find God. Being a bloodhound for good helps us discover how God acts in our world and how God is working in our own life. Or to paraphrase Paul's words, "If you keep on looking for good, if you keep on doing the things I have taught, God will be with you." Or as Nick Carter the bloodhound might put it, "Keep your noses clean and keep sniffing out the good."

Is your nose trained to pick up the good? Do you keep your eyes open to find the best in others? Do you go to worship looking for ways to praise

God and praise the good; or do you go as though judging a talent contest, giving the choir, the soloist, the pastor, the reader, and the preacher marks from one to ten? Are you so busy looking for the 10 percent that isn't perfect that you miss the 90 percent that is good and helpful? Are you so concerned with how others are doing that you miss the chance for the Spirit to be doing something in your own life?

How are you doing in your relationships? Do you have a nose that sniffs out the good in your family, among your friends, and in all the places you frequent at work? Are you intentional about spending time and effort looking for ways to encourage others? Do you pick up the subtle smells of God's grace and forgiveness along the way? Are you one who will "stay on the trail" searching until you have found the last speck of evidence that tells us God is working in and among God's people? If not, how about putting your nose to work today? Be a bloodhound for God. Find good. Find God.

To make this devotion your own:

• Tell about a person who comes to mind when you think of a "bloodhound for good," someone who consistently looks for the good in others.

• Share ways you find God in the good, the beautiful, the true, the honorable.

• Think about areas where you might start sniffing out the good—looking for the positive—in your church, your neighborhood, and your home.

Challenge

God is our refuge and strength,
an ever-present help in trouble.
(Psalm 46:1 NIV)

In the early 1900s this challenge was placed in a London newspaper in the form of an advertisement: "Men wanted for hazardous journey. Small wages, bitter cold, long hours of complete darkness, constant danger, safe return doubtful. Honor and recognition in case of success . . . " The response to the ad was so great that many were turned away. The advertiser was Sir Ernest Shackleton, and his objective was to gather together a group of men to explore the Antarctic. He knew the secret of motivation is to challenge others. And it's a principle that still works wonders today.

Certainly Jesus challenged his followers. It wasn't going to be easy to be a disciple. Death and persecution were two of the many hazards of telling others about Jesus. And in many parts of the world today, following Jesus has not become any easier. There is a high cost to be a believer. It is a challenge, however, that many people accept because the Holy Spirit has given them the power to persevere.

We are told that challenges work because they move us from the ordinary into the world of the extraordinary. If the challenge appeals to a dream or a special interest, people are drawn to it. People want to be involved in something that makes a difference, that influences others positively. As Christians, our rewards can be eternal because our words and deeds can further God's kingdom. And the biggest challenge is that there is so much to be done.

In our busy world, it can be a challenge just to take the time to really listen to someone or to offer some appreciation for a job well done. In God's world, the little things can be the big things. Our hands, heart, feet, and ears can be instruments of God, used to solve the toughest challenges. We may not be asked to travel to faraway lands. Often God wants us to bloom where we are planted.

It has been said that leadership is action, not position. We can all do our part in accepting the challenges God gives us and in challenging others to a more effective and dynamic ministry.

To make this devotion your own:

• Share how you have been challenged to reach a goal.
• Review some of the challenges facing your congregation.
• Share what motivates you to meet daily challenges.

Cheering

Some nations boast of their armies and weapons,
but we boast in the LORD our God.
(Psalm 20:7 NLT)

You don't hear many people cheering or boasting about God these days. If you look at God's credentials, there's plenty to boast and cheer about. Let's see—all knowing, all powerful, all present, created the entire universe and still does a pretty good job of keeping things going, won battles for people outnumbered ten thousand to one, came to earth as a human being to be one of us, died for us, forgives us our sins and gives us everlasting life, gives each of us the power of the Holy Spirit, comes to us through the Bible and prayer, heals us when we're sick, and will never leave us nor forsake us. If you look at the facts objectively, God has a pretty good record—in fact, the best in the business.

Outside of Sunday worship, however, you don't hear many people cheering or boasting about the awesome God we have the privilege to worship and follow and love. Have you ever heard anyone bragging about God? Can you imagine the conversations there would be if we replaced God with the usual things we boast about? Can you imagine if houses, the opposite sex, cars, jobs, athletic teams, kids, and other things worth talking about were replaced with boasting and cheering about God? Wouldn't that be—well, different?

"Some boast of chariots and some of horses, but our boast is in the name of the LORD our God" (Psalm 20:7 NLT). The people of Israel knew who was in charge. They didn't always act like it, but they knew God was their source and life. And it wasn't a private, individual thing, either. They boasted about God as a nation. They gathered together for days to cheer about the things God had done for them. Together they worshiped and believed and called on their God. And God always responded.

How about you? In terms of your faith, is your first reaction to cheer or boast about God? Is the first thing on your mind or off your tongue to declare God's praises? If not, why not? Why shouldn't we brag about God? If someone you knew was on a team in the state championship playoffs, would you simply stay quiet? Or would you clap and cheer and boast a little about the one you knew on the team?

In what armies or weapons do you boast? On what do you rely? With what do you trust your life? When it comes to battle, on what or whom do you call? Is it the army of plenty? Is it the weapon of self-reliance? Or is it simply yourself in whom you place your trust?

We have a great God. We have a God who knows each of us personally, a God who has fashioned and formed us and made us and claimed us as his own. May our cheers, may our life, join with the psalmist in saying, "some nations boast of their armies and weapons, but we boast in the LORD our God."

To make this devotion your own:

• Think of something or someone you boasted about when you were growing up.
• Share ways in which you boast about God, ways in which you praise and thank God for all he has done for you.
• Tell about a time when God did something in your own life about which you could boast.

Comparisons

Then the mother of the sons of Zebedee came to him with her sons, and kneeling before him, she asked a favor of him. And he said to her, "What do you want?" She said to him, "Declare that these two sons of mine will sit, one at your right hand and one at your left, in your kingdom." But Jesus answered, "You do not know what you are asking. Are you able to drink the cup that I am about to drink?" They said to him, "We are able." He said to them, "You will indeed drink my cup, but to sit at my right hand and at my left, this is not mine to grant, but it is for those for whom it has been prepared by my Father."

When the ten heard it, they were angry with the two brothers. But Jesus called them to him and said, "You know that the rulers of the Gentiles LORD it over them, and their great ones are tyrants over them. It will not be so among you; but whoever wishes to be great among you must be your servant, and whoever wishes to be first among you must be your slave; just as the Son of Man came not to be served but to serve, and to give his life a ransom for many."

(Matthew 20:20-28)

Comparison rarely brings out the best in others.

You've experienced it yourself, haven't you? Someone who has known your brother or sister or father or mother or second cousin twice removed greets you with the words, "You don't look a thing like your mother." Or "You don't talk like your brother." Or "You play football like your Aunt Edna."

Comparison rarely brings out the best in others. Think of your own life for a minute. Has a comparison ever brought out the best in you? Has it helped you excel, has it motivated you to a higher purpose, has it helped you become a better person? Has comparison ever helped you achieve and strive for anything? Comparison rarely brings out the best in others because someone always loses in a comparison; and if anything, it becomes an excuse to be less than we could be and less than what God intended us to be. "Oh, well," it's easy to rationalize, "if I can't be as good as Simon the Saint, why bother at all even trying?"

Comparison didn't bring out the best in the disciples, either. When they heard the request of James and John's mother to have her sons sit next to Jesus in his kingdom, "they were angry with the two brothers" (Matthew 20:24). They must have thought, How can they ask for such special privileges? How can they ask for the two seats of highest honor in God's kingdom, right next to Jesus? Do they think they're better than we are? We're just as good as they are.

Jesus knew how destructive comparisons were and moved immediately from comparison to an attitude of service. "Whoever wishes to be great among you must be your servant, and whoever wishes to be first among you must be your slave; just as the Son of Man came not to be served but to serve, and to give his life a ransom for many" (Matthew 20:26-28).

God doesn't compare us to others. God doesn't expect us to be someone we are not. God doesn't withhold his healing or forgiveness for a more deserving moment. God doesn't wait to love us until we are as good as you-know-who. No, God doesn't compare us to others; God simply loves us just as we are.

To make this devotion your own:

• Think of a time you were compared with someone else. How did it make you feel?
• Share whether you agree with the author that God loves each of us now, just as we are.
• Reflect on how God's love has allowed you to change or given you the freedom to change.

Contentment

—◦◦◦—

A cheerful heart is a good medicine,
but a downcast spirit dries up the bones.
(Proverbs 17:22)

You may not remember the name Fanny Crosby, but you probably have read one of her religious poems, some of which have become hymns. In her lifetime Fanny wrote more than seven hundred poems about God and her faith. Her very first poem began with these words:

> Oh, what a happy soul I am,
> Although I cannot see,
> I am resolved that in this world
> Contented I will be.

That's right, Fanny was blind from age six until her death at age eighty-eight, but that never prevented her from praising God and being happy with life. Fanny was one of those rare individuals who rose above her troubles and found peace and contentment with her world. Her faith in God helped her be thankful for what she had, while bringing joy to the lives of others.

Fanny knew the secret to contentment. She had problems, just like everyone else; but she discovered that problems can only affect your life to the point you let them affect your thinking. God has not given us freedom from problems, but God has given us freedom of choice. How we respond to the challenges we face is completely up to us. It is a matter of attitude.

Contentment in life is an acquired talent, a gift from God that begins with faith. If we believe in a God who loves us, the troubles of this world are not so scary. Our faith does make a difference in how we look at life. We are secure because God is our security. We are content because we put our trust in God. We have a purpose in life because we know God placed us on earth to serve him. A strong faith not only helps answer life's toughest questions, it also leads us to contentment.

Worry, self-pity, and despair can all be part of life. We all have our

33

troubles. Some people may have lesser problems than you face; other people have heavier burdens. The key, however, is how we respond to the cards we are dealt. And how we respond determines our contentment.

As Fanny learned early in life, it is not what we lack but what we have that counts. A strong faith, coupled with daily prayer, can give us the peace we seek. Life is a matter of choices.

To make this devotion your own:

• Share what brings you contentment.
• Discuss how you make choices or how your attitude affects your life.
• Talk about why you selected this devotion to share.

Control

Unless you change and become like little children, you will never enter the kingdom of heaven.

(Matthew 18:3 NIV)

We like to be in control. Think about it for a minute.

We control our diet.

We control our exercise.

We control our cholesterol.

We control our blood pressure.

We control our finances.

We try to control our temper.

We control the temperature in our houses.

We control the temperature in our cars—sometimes even both sides of the car.

How many times were you controlled this weekend or even this morning as you paused at stoplights, stop signs, pedestrian crossings, bus stops, or ramp meters?

And as if controlling our immediate surroundings isn't enough, we can now control our environments without even being there. We can control our environment from a distance, from a remote location. We change channels on our TV from another room using the remote control. Think of all the little skirmishes throughout the living rooms and dens of the United States just to see who ends up with the remote! We open garage doors a half block away. We can operate our office computers remotely from home. We can start our cars in the garage by pushing a button while we are still inside the house. We can move our offices into our cars by using cell phones, faxes, and pagers. We operate satellites and space probes from millions of miles away.

We like to be in control, yet we pay dearly to have this control. How much have you or your spouse or your company spent, in one way or another, on time management to gain control of those pesky minutes? How much time and energy have you spent on food, on diets, on nutrition, just to gain some control over your current weight? How about time and energy to control the kids or the dog or the neighbors next door? How much thought and effort did you spend today simply to control the few things you could control in your hectic schedule? No doubt about it, we like to be in control.

When Jesus said we are to change and become like children, he didn't mean that we should somehow recover a childlike innocence. Instead, Jesus calls us to remember how dependent children are on their parents' love and trust, how they look to their parents to take care of them, to protect them, to nurture them; how they look first to their parents to supply their needs rather than to themselves.

What is your first reaction when you confront a situation where you feel out of control? Do you immediately give control of the situation to God, or do you start clawing to regain control? Do you plan how you will live your life, or do you give control of each situation to God? Jesus calls us to look to God for our every need. Jesus calls us to let God take control of our lives. Jesus calls us to trust God in all situations. Jesus invites us to become like children, to trust our loving Parent with every detail in our lives.

So go ahead—lose control. Let the Spirit take over your life. Give your problems and frustrations and headaches over to God. Lose control, and begin to discover the wonderful kingdom of God.

To make this devotion your own:

• Share a situation when things felt out of control for you.
• Tell about a time you experienced God's peace in the midst of losing control.
• Reflect on ways you've struggled to give control of your life over to God.

Crime

===◊◊◊===

Do not be overcome by evil, but overcome evil with good.
(Romans 12:21 NIV)

In a crime-infested neighborhood in an inner city, a window in an old house displays this sign: "God is watching you. He loves you so much that he can't take his eyes off you." Is the sign an effort at crime prevention or a testimony to the love of God? Maybe it's a bit of both.

We live in a world that is at war. It seems we are often unwilling spectators in a battle between good and evil. The media give us daily updates on how the battle is going. The news often contains details of murder, rape, arson, burglary, theft, hate crimes, and vandalism. Often we hold our breath, pray, and hope that we do not become victims of crime.

What perhaps scares people most is the uncertainty. A trip to the grocery store can end in a car jacking. A child playing in the front yard can be the unintended victim of a drive-by shooting. A burglar could be entering your home this minute. We have reason to be afraid and uncertain. Life offers few guarantees. Our world seems to be changing, and sometimes it seems that it is not changing for the better.

The good news is that God is with us in the midst of our fear. God can protect us from harm. Daily a God who does take an active role in protecting his people delivers us from evil. God guarantees his presence. We may not understand why bad things happen to good people, but we trust in a God who never lets us out of his sight. We trust that God has things under control and that we are eternally in his care.

Crime is a fact of life, and we may at times be a victim of it. That is life. It is not how God intended, nor how he desires us to live. God does want us to be safe, but God is not solely in the business of fighting crime. God is in the business of loving people, wanting to develop a relationship with them, and desiring to have everyone come to know the love of Jesus Christ.

Is there an answer to crime? Perhaps it is simply what the sign in the window reminds us about God. He is watching. And he loves us so much that he can't take his eyes off us. That's eternal protection.

To make this devotion your own:

• Share how crime has affected your life.
• Discuss ideas you have about helping crime victims or preventing crime.
• Talk about local crimes that are currently in the news.

Dreams

=◉◉◉=

Now the boy Samuel was ministering to the LORD under Eli. The word of the LORD was rare in those days; visions were not widespread. At that time Eli, whose eyesight had begun to grow dim so that he could not see, was lying down in his room; the lamp of God had not yet gone out, and Samuel was lying down in the temple of the LORD, where the ark of God was. Then the LORD called, "Samuel! Samuel!" and he said, "Here I am!" and ran to Eli, and said, "Here I am, for you called me." But he said, "I did not call; lie down again." So he went and lay down. The LORD called again, "Samuel!" Samuel got up and went to Eli, and said, "Here I am, for you called me." But he said, "I did not call, my son; lie down again." Now Samuel did not yet know the LORD, and the word of the LORD had not yet been revealed to him. The LORD called Samuel again, a third time. And he got up and went to Eli, and said, "Here I am, for you called me." Then Eli perceived that the LORD was calling the boy. Therefore Eli said to Samuel, "Go, lie down; and if he calls you, you shall say, 'Speak, LORD, for your servant is listening.'"

(1 Samuel 3:1-9)

Rick Hanson was named Canadian Athlete of the Year with hockey great Wayne Gretsky in 1983. His future looked hopeful until an auto accident shortly afterward severed his spinal cord and left him confined to a wheelchair.

Rick was not going to let a physical disability sap his life and hope, however. He had a dream while recuperating from that devastating experience. He was going to be the first person ever to traverse the world in a wheelchair.

Rick began a crusade of riding so that others with disabilities, both mental and physical, might also grab hold of a dream and do something positive. He rode his wheelchair through the blizzards of the Canadian winter, the heat of the Arizona deserts, and the ups and downs of the Great Wall of China.

After several years of riding, Rick finished his dream in May of 1987. He had traveled a total of more than 27,000 miles. As he was welcomed back into his hometown in Canada, his one hope among refrains of joyous tears was that others might start building their own dreams as he had, no matter how small the dreams were.

Some people think dreams are unrealistic. If you think about it, however, everything begins with a dream. Electricity and flying and space travel were merely dreams before people decided to help make them real. The skyscraper is first dreamed of in a person's imagination years before it is completed as a building. Rick Hanson's goal to ride around the world in a wheelchair began as a dream long before he began making his worldwide trek. In fact, the dream was the spark that ignited the fire so that Rick could pursue his dream. Yes, everything great begins first as a dream.

As Christians, one of our responsibilities is to inspire others to dream. Like Eli telling the young boy Samuel to listen to the Lord's call in his own dream, we can encourage those around us to listen to the heartbeat of God in their lives. We can help others work toward their call of serving others, even as we serve with them.

What is your dream for your church, your community, or the world? What small thing can you do today to work toward that dream? How can you inspire others to fulfill their visions? Does it mean listening more closely to God in your own life? Could it be inviting a friend to worship? How about a daily commitment to Bible reading or prayer to listen more closely to God?

"Dreams are the touchstones of our characters," wrote Henry David Thoreau. Inspiring others to dream touches not only our own life but also the lives of others. So keep those dreams before you, and nurture those dreams in others. May we, like Samuel, be open to the work of the Lord as we respond, "Here I am Lord, speak."

To make this devotion your own:

- Share ways you were either encouraged, or discouraged, to dream as a child.
- Think of a dream you have for the future. How will God help you accomplish it?
- Reflect on ways we can trust God to help us accomplish our dreams or goals.

Duet

Therefore, my beloved, just as you have always obeyed me, not only in my presence, but much more now in my absence, work out your own salvation with fear and trembling; for it is God who is at work in you, enabling you both to will and to work for his good pleasure.

(Philippians 2:12-13)

The eight-year-old boy sat impatiently next to his mother as they waited for the world-renowned pianist to take center stage and start playing. The excited mother, who was engaged in conversation with those around her, hadn't noticed that the youngster had slipped away. The sudden gasps and surprised comments that erupted from the crowd moved the mother's head toward center stage. There, sitting on the piano bench, was her son. To her horror and the horror of the crowd, he began plucking out the tune "Twinkle, Twinkle, Little Star."

Of course, the crowd did not know what to do. Their gaping mouths and painful looks waited for a quick resolution to this predicament.

Without a word, the world-renowned pianist quietly walked on stage, motioning for the audience to take their seats and to be quiet. He walked behind the young boy, who was still playing at this time, and added a simple but melodic base line with his left hand. When the surprised youngster looked back, the master simply nodded for the boy to keep playing, and in a few moments added a beautiful contrapuntal melody with his right hand. Back and forth, back and forth, student and master continued the musical exchange, and for the next hour the crowd sat mesmerized. What began as a simple archaic melody had been transformed into a masterpiece.

This is how God works in our world. To our simple and archaic melodies, God breathes new life. When the rest of the world gasps at the simplicity in how we view the world, God stands behind us and guides us, giving us the wisdom and direction and help we need to do God's will. When others wait for someone else to get involved and take action, God nudges us and transforms us with the beautiful melody of grace, forgiveness, and mercy. God transforms our stark, black and white world into a colorful variation of life and love.

41

We are all amateurs, really. We are fragile, sinful human beings. But God has come into our lives to make us more, much more. God has come into our lives to remind us that each person is a masterpiece in God's care. Each person is God's handiwork, created to give hope and life to others as God works within us.

To make this devotion your own:

• Reflect on whether your first inclination is to play a solo by yourself or play a duet with God.
• Share a way in which God has helped you use one of your gifts.
• Tell those with whom you are sharing this devotion the gifts they have and how you see them using those gifts with God's help.

Epitaphs

I thank my God every time I remember you.
(Philippians 1:3 NIV)

There is a site on the Internet called findagrave.com that allows you to visit the graves of famous people all over the world. The site often provides a photo of the grave, gives the date of birth and death, and can even draw you a map of the cemetery where the person is buried. Some of the graves of these famous people are simple. Others are elaborate monuments of stone. What many find most interesting, however, are the epitaphs carved in the gravestones. The grave of Dean Martin has the words, "Everybody Loves Somebody Sometime." Jackie Gleason's epitaph is "And Away We Go!" while Roy Rogers has "The Cowboy's Prayer."

Whether or not people are famous, all leave behind an epitaph when they die. Some epitaphs are written in stone, but many are written in the hearts of people who knew and loved them. While a gravestone only indicates the date of birth and death, it is what a person did between those years that matters the most.

In birth and death we arrive and depart alone. We bring nothing with us into life. When death comes, we take nothing with us. The possessions we leave behind go to new owners. The only thing we take to our grave is our legacy.

We are remembered in death by what we did or did not do in life. Acts of love continue to live after we are gone. Only loved ones keep our memory alive. The organizations and causes we supported are often monuments to our years on earth. Memorials given to churches, to hospitals, and toward research for diseases are another way we are remembered.

Life has been called a rat race, a feast, a predicament, and many other things; but it is certainly a priceless gift from God. And the best gifts are shared with others during our lifetime. How will you be remembered? Your epitaph is written by your words and deeds today.

To make this devotion your own:

• Talk about someone you loved who has died.
• Share why you selected this topic for a devotion.
• Discuss the different ways we remember loved ones.

Faith

For truly I tell you, if you have faith the size of a mustard seed, you will say to this mountain, "Move from here to there," and it will move; and nothing will be impossible for you.

(Matthew 17:20)

Imagine you are crossing a desert by foot. You are out of water. Your throat is dry. And then you come across a tin can, containing a letter, that sits next to an old pump. The following letter contains your only hope for water:

"This pump is all right as of June 1932. I put a new washer into it and it ought to last many years, but the washer dries out and the pump has got to be primed. Under the white rock I buried a bottle of water, out of the sun and cork end up. There's enough water to prime the pump, but not if you drink some first. Pour about one fourth and let her soak to wet the leather. Then you pour in the rest medium fast and pump like crazy. You'll get water. The well has never run dry. Have faith. When you get watered up, fill the bottle and put it back like you found it for the next feller.—Desert Pete

P.S. Don't go drinking up the water first. Prime the pump with it, and you'll get all you can hold."

Now comes the tough question. Would you prime the pump or drink the water?

It's a question of faith. It is much like the faith we take for granted on a daily basis. We have faith each day that our car will work properly, that the sun will rise, that a lamp will light when we turn on a light switch, and that the computer we rely on—but don't understand—will not crash.

The Christian faith is not about things; it is about God and our relationship with him. We have faith that there is a living God, who knows us personally, loves us, provides for us, and will give us eternal life. We worship this God out of love for all he has done for us. We have never seen our God, but in our soul we know he exists, as sure as the air that we breathe.

It is our faith in Christ that makes it possible for us to live. When we pray, we have faith that God hears us and answers our prayer. When we

45

read the Bible, we have faith that it is the word of God. Our religion is empty and meaningless without faith. It is the glue that keeps us together and connects us with God.

The creed we read in church and the hymns we sing there are based on faith. Some Christians have more faith than others do. Those who have not been transformed by the gospel may have no faith in God at all. They may have only faith in themselves. And faith is different from hope. Hope is like a wish, but faith is trust in a living God.

Take time to remember the importance of your faith today. Continue to nurture it. In the words of Saint Augustine, "Seek not to understand that you may believe, but believe that you may understand." This is the essence of faith.

To make this devotion your own:

• Talk about the people and life experiences that have shaped your faith.
• Share how your faith is nurtured.
• Discuss what your faith means to you.

Fear

Do not be afraid. . . .I am your shield.
(Genesis 15:1 NIV)

"Has Jesus forgotten me? Does he know where I live?" It was a question a ninety-nine-year-old mother asked her daughter. Lillian has been in a nursing home for more than a decade. Her weight has declined to about seventy-five pounds, she has lost her eyesight, and her hearing is marginal. Her daughter, who visits her daily, assures Lillian that God is with her; he hasn't forgotten. Lillian continues to wait for Jesus to take her home.

My God, why have you forsaken me? It is a question we all ask at one time or another. It is human to be afraid, to doubt, and to wonder where God is when we need him. We want God to calm our fears and to deliver us from the troubles of this world. In times of darkness we seek his light and reassurance that we are not alone. We cry out for God, and we wait for an answer.

"Do not be afraid; I am your shield." It is more than an answer. It is God's promise to us. Nothing can separate us from God's love.

Fear is real, but it is no match for God. The troubles that face us at work, at home, during the day, or in our hearts in the quiet of a sleepless night are temporary bumps in the road of life. In the big picture of things, God holds everything in the palm of his hand. God has conquered sin, death, and the power of the devil through the death and resurrection of Jesus.

If you are feeling anxious about what the future holds, look to the God of the past, present, and future. In the past God blessed and preserved you. He has kept you safe. In the present, God is with you through prayer and in the pages of the Bible. In the future and through eternity, you belong to God. Turn your fears over to him. God will show you the way.

Psalm 27:1 says it best. It answers our questions with a question. "The LORD is my light and my salvation; whom shall I fear?"

To make this devotion your own:

• Discuss a time in your life when you were afraid and share how God helped you overcome your fear.
• Share what prompted you to select this devotion and how it helped you.
• Discuss your views on the fears of children or the fears of the elderly and how God provides peace.

Fishing

And Jesus said to them, "Follow me and I will make you fish for people."
(Mark 1:17)

The story is told that Mark Twain, returning from a fishing trip, was bragging to a stranger about his success. Twain told the man about catching dozens of bass in a lake where fishing was not permitted. The stranger was quite interested in the story and introduced himself as the local game warden. Thinking quickly, Twain asked if the stranger knew who he was. The stranger did not know Twain, who introduced himself as the biggest liar in the United States.

It seems everybody has a fishing story to tell. Stories range from the fish that got away to that secret spot where the fish are always biting. People enjoy fishing because of the peace and quiet on the lake and because the unexpected can happen; you never know what you might catch.

It's not surprising then why Jesus chose some fishermen to be his disciples. Jesus was going to make them "fishers of men" so his story would be known throughout the world. The first disciples had two fishing skills: patience and perseverance needed to get the job done.

As Christ's disciples today, we can use those same fishing skills to bring others to Christ. Our bait is the good news of a God who loves us and the joy of having a personal relationship with Christ. Whether we "fish" at work or in our own neighborhood, the gospel is our anchor as we share what Christ means to us.

In a world that is hungry for the bread of life, bringing others to Christ can be a rewarding experience that changes lives. You can begin by inviting others to church. Ask God to present opportunities to talk about your faith. Prepare by reading the Bible and praying. Creativity and ingenuity are other tools of today's disciples.

God loves the people of this world so much that he wants everyone to know about Jesus. Now it's up to us to share the good news.

To make this devotion your own:

• Share your ideas on how fishing and discipleship are related.

• Tell about a time where you talked about your faith while fishing.

• Discuss why the mission of the church is so important to you.

Gifts

Every generous act of giving, with every perfect gift, is from above.
                                                               (James 1:17)

Jim Anderson lived in a small town in the Midwest. The year was 1931 and times were bad. It was the time of the Great Depression. Food and jobs were scarce. Most people were out of work. Survival was a struggle. One morning Jim stepped out on his porch to discover a small basket of food with a few dollar bills tucked in the side. His discovery delighted and puzzled him at the same time. Who was his mysterious benefactor and why was he chosen to receive such goodness? Jim kept the receipt of the gift to himself and told no one.

The next day, it happened again. The basket containing food for the day and a few dollars was sitting on his porch. Morning after morning Jim was blessed with food and a few dollars. He even tried to stay up all night and watch his porch to see who his benefactor was. Jim never saw anyone, but his basket continued to appear. And Jim continued to keep all this a secret. He never told a soul.

Weeks went by and one day Jim made a discovery. Quite by accident he found out that all his neighbors, in fact everyone in the entire town, were also receiving a basket of food and dollars each morning. This news devastated Jim. Now that he knew he was not special, Jim began to resent the baskets his neighbors were being given. His resentment did not stop him from continuing to receive a basket each day, but it certainly spoiled his pleasure.

How often we forget that each of us is also sustained daily by a "mysterious benefactor" who provides for all our daily needs. The gifts are countless and arrive day after day with no strings attached. Food, clothing, health, employment, home, transportation, entertainment, the beauty of nature are just some of the many gifts we receive but often take for granted. We are given the gift of life and years of time on this earth. And how we use our "free" time is completely up to us! Our benefactor attaches few restrictions.

What does our benefactor want from us? He wants to have a

relationship. We already have his love, a promise of eternal life, daily protection, and more. And he accepts us just the way we are and forgives us when we do wrong. That is quite a friend indeed!

Looking for a benefactor? You already have one. His name is Jesus, and he loves you so much he died on the cross for you. Let him know today how much you appreciate his many gifts and goodness!

To make this devotion your own:

• Share why you think we take God and his blessings for granted.
• Discuss some of the many gifts you have received from God.
• Use a basket of food as a prop for leading this devotion.

Good Ol' Days

As for me, I am poor and needy,
but the Lord is thinking about me right now.
You are my helper and my savior.
Do not delay, O my God.
(Psalm 40:17 NLT)

Nothing like it had ever happened before. Never had people been so dependent on one resource for lighting, food, heating, and energy. This resource, once thought to have an unlimited supply, was within a year or two of being depleted forever. The *Boston Globe* reflected the sentiment of the general public when it ran the following headline in the 1850s: "World to go dark! Whale oil scarce!"

It was the mid-1970s. People waited in lines for hours simply to fill their gas tanks. The recession, skyrocketing gas prices, gas rationing, OPEC, the nuclear arms race with Russia, and the energy crisis made the future look bleak at best. What was the world coming to? Things had never been this bad before. Back in the good ol' days...

High school shootings in Littleton, Colorado. A homemade truck bomb in Omaha, Nebraska. One tragedy after another awakens a new fear in us. What is this world coming to, we wonder? When is it all going to stop? Things like this never happened before... did they? We may feel like the psalmist who laments,

> Troubles surround me—
> too many to count!
> They pile up so high
> I can't see my way out.
> They are more numerous than the hairs on my head.
> I have lost all my courage. (Psalm 40:12 NLT)

It is easy, and perhaps natural, to think that times were always better before, back in the good ol' days. But were things really better in the past? Was it really a better time to live during the Great Depression, or the two

53

world wars, or the civil rights atrocities, or the polio epidemics, or the Korean and Vietnam wars, or the Cold War, or the nuclear arms race? Were times really better in the good ol' days? Or are the good ol' days right now, at this moment? The psalmist gives us a clue. Just a few verses after his heart-wrenching lament of overwhelming problems he writes,

> As for me, I am poor and needy,
>> but the LORD is thinking about me right now.
> You are my helper and my savior.
>> Do not delay, O my God. (Psalm 40:17 NLT)

Despite all that surrounds him, the focus of the psalmist is on the present. "The LORD is thinking about me right now. You are my helper and my savior. Do not delay, O my God." The answer to his struggles did not reside in a more peaceful past or in another situation. The answer to his struggles rested in God. The answer to his struggles rested in the present. The answer to his struggles rested not in a particular time in history but in a particular being, namely God.

So too the answer to our struggles lies with our "helper and savior." The answer to our current struggles rests not in going back to some better time in the past, but in looking to God now, in the present. The best times are here and now, because it is here and now that God is in our midst. It is here and now that God is with us in all situations. It is here and now, in the midst of all that surrounds us, that God is most visible and where God can act most powerfully. "The LORD is thinking about me right now. You are my helper and my savior. Do not delay, O my God."

To make this devotion your own:

- Tell what comes to mind for you when you think of the "good ol' days."
- Think of reasons today is a great time to be alive in the world.
- Reflect on ways we can trust in God right now to make each day the best day ever.

Harvesting

That same day Jesus went out of the house and sat beside the sea. Such great crowds gathered around him that he got into a boat and sat there, while the whole crowd stood on the beach. And he told them many things in parables, saying: "Listen! A sower went out to sow. And as he sowed, some seeds fell on the path, and the birds came and ate them up. Other seeds fell on rocky ground, where they did not have much soil, and they sprang up quickly, since they had no depth of soil. But when the sun rose, they were scorched; and since they had no root, they withered away. Other seeds fell among thorns, and the thorns grew up and choked them. Other seeds fell on good soil and brought forth grain, some a hundredfold, some sixty, some thirty. Let anyone with ears listen!"

(Matthew 13:1-9)

There is something basic and good about being a farmer. Getting in touch with the earth, being aware of the yearly cycles, getting your hands dirty, working by the sun's clock, looking over a vast empty field of opportunity, seeing your efforts come to fruition. Some people might think farmers simply plant, then reap. But in reality they plant, they wait, they wait, they wait, and then if everything goes right, they reap.

This is not a parable about instant gratification. It is not about planting one day and reaping a harvest twenty-four hours later. This is not a retelling of the story of Jack and the Beanstalk, where magic seeds sprout and grow heavenward in the span of one night's rest. Rather, this parable is the reality of what happens in life and what happens to seeds planted, all with the best intention. Some seeds never find fertile ground. Other seeds grow quickly at first, but soon die out. Still others grow but never reach their full potential. And then there are a few seeds that actually take root and thrive in the good soil. Just a few good seeds bring forth a harvest of thirty to a hundredfold. You plant, you wait, you wait, you wait; and then if everything goes right, you reap.

Such is the case in our lives of faith. While we'd like to see immediate, gratifying results (the Jack-and-the-beanstalk syndrome), planting and preparing and waiting for seed to grow is hard work. It is not very satisfying. Results do not pop up overnight. Often, results take a lifetime. Results are not instantaneous. For example, the time and energy spent raising kids does not always bear visible fruit in the days and weeks ahead. Going the extra mile at work or with coworkers does not show up in the next paycheck. Starting an intentional prayer life one day does not guarantee that the next day will be a day full of miracles, or that we will take our place with saints past. Halos do not come easily, nor do they come quickly. There is always time between sowing and reaping, planting and harvesting. There is waiting. Of course Jesus knew this. He grew up and was surrounded by the cycles of sowing and reaping and waiting.

In terms of our faith and in terms of our own efforts, we may do the sowing, but God takes care of the reaping. No matter how much we'd like to think our planted seeds were magical, it takes time and it takes God to bring about the abundant harvest. If we plant a seed one day and dig it up the next day to see how it's doing, we will destroy it. Yes, we are responsible for the planting; but God, in time, will take care of the harvest. We plant, we wait, we wait, we wait, and then if everything goes right, God reaps.

Our actions, our seeds, are merely ways by which the Spirit has opportunity to work. They are not everything. They are the seeds God uses to begin new life. Through the Spirit God develops those tiny little seeds, after much waiting, into an abundant harvest.

To make this devotion your own:

• Tell an experience you've had in terms of planting and harvesting.
• Discuss ways God has used others to plant seeds of faith in your own life.
• Think of ways you can plant positive, faith-filled seeds in the lives of others.

Heaven

In my Father's house are many rooms; if it were not so, I would have told you. I am going there to prepare a place for you.

(John 14:2 NIV)

The story is told of an army chaplain who was walking a convicted cattle rustler to the gallows to be hanged. On the way, the chaplain said to the rustler, "Things will be much better for you in heaven."

"Do you really believe that?" asked the rustler.

"Why, yes I do," replied the chaplain.

"Then switch places with me," said the rustler, "because I like it here."

No matter how attractive heaven sounds, most people prefer life on earth. We want to go to heaven, but are in no hurry to get there. On earth we have our friends, family, and generally the basics of life. Life is good for most of us. Why leave behind what we know and love for a place we know little about? Such a long distance move is scary, especially since you have to die to go to heaven.

The transition between life on earth and life in heaven has sometimes been compared to being born. Imagine a contented baby in a mother's womb. The baby has food, protection and a good life. In the birth process, everything changes. The known is left behind for the unknown. A new world suddenly appears. Given a choice in the matter, the baby would probably prefer to stay in the womb. Why give up a sure thing for a strange new world? In a way, birth and death are similar. We have no choice and must experience both adventures.

God loves us and eventually wants us to go to heaven to be with him. However, he has first given each of us the gift of life and things to do and learn on earth. God has big plans for us. We have people to meet, places to go, and challenges to meet. Our spiritual lives must be developed. Life on earth is a time of becoming acquainted with God. We grow in faith until we are ready for a brand new experience and a brand new world called heaven.

What is heaven like? We know God is there with all the saints. It is a place without pain and hardship, where God will meet all our needs.

Heaven represents peace and happiness. Jesus says that a mansion is prepared for us. And we know that heaven is forever. It's our final destination where we are united with God and our loved ones.

For many of us, heaven can wait. We love life. But all life does come to an end. And that's where heaven begins.

To make this devotion your own:

• Share your own thoughts about heaven.
• Talk about how people fear change and the unknown.
• Discuss your thoughts about God's purpose for us on earth.

Journey

I meditate on your age-old laws;
O LORD, they comfort me.
I am furious with the wicked,
those who reject your law.
Your principles have been the music of my life
Throughout the years of my pilgrimage.
I reflect at night on who you are, O LORD,
and I obey your law because of this.
This is my happy way of life:
obeying your commandments.
                              (Psalm 119:52-56 NLT)

Unfortunately, people don't learn everything they need to know in kindergarten. It would be nice if they did, but don't you feel safer on the roads knowing that other adults, not grade-schoolers, are behind the wheels of cars? While we can reapply some of the knowledge we gained in kindergarten, learning is really a lifelong process. Learning is an ever-changing journey.

The psalmist sees faith as a lifelong journey, a process of growth. "Your principles have been the music of my life throughout the years of my pilgrimage," he says (verse 54). This isn't someone who has learned about God's law in an instant and remembered it all. Nor is it about someone who has forgotten about God's law. This is someone who has learned God's law and put it to heart, someone who daily reflects on how God's word will make life more meaningful and enjoyable. In short, this is someone who sees faith as a lifelong journey.

Have you ever wondered why churches offer Bible studies for adults? Have you ever wondered why we read the same Bible over and over again? Have you ever wondered why you basically hear the same gospel message every week in the sermon; it's just told fifty-two different ways each year? While we may have learned the basic truths of everything we needed to know about our faith in Sunday school, life is different as adults. The working world presents us with different problems and opportunities than did the classroom. Our bosses are not always as understanding or patient as some of our teachers once were. Our situations are different. We cannot respond the same way we did in kindergarten. Crying for attention as an adult just doesn't have the impact it did as a child. Our situations are different. We are on a journey, a never-ending experience of learning.

Think about your life for a moment. Have you run into situations that have stretched your thinking? Have you been more honest with who you are as a person, more honest with your human capacity for sin, with your longing to be your own god, or with your desire to be in control of your own situation? On the other hand, how have you experienced God's grace and love? How have you seen lives changed through the power of the Holy Spirit? In what ways have you encountered miracles where you knew beyond a shadow of a doubt God was working? What things have you learned now that made absolutely no sense in your youth?

Our life of faith is a journey. Each day is a new opportunity to discover how much God loves us, how hard God is working in the world to save all people, the great extent of God's forgiveness, and the special creation God made in you. These concepts may take years to learn and understand. It doesn't happen in a vacuum, however, or come to us simply because we get older. It comes as we keep God's word in front of us day in and day out. It comes as we open ourselves daily to God's work and God's Spirit. It comes as we struggle on a daily basis with the ways God calls and loves and forgives us.

To make this devotion your own:

• Think of a journey you've taken. What did you enjoy most about it?
• Share ways in which your life of faith has been a journey, a process of learning over the years.
• Choose a word or phrase from the psalm above and share why it is meaningful to you.

Kindness

I will recount the gracious deeds of the LORD,
the praiseworthy acts of the LORD,
because of all that the LORD has done for us.

(Isaiah 63:7)

Author Barbara J. Winter tells the story of an act of unexpected kindness that happened to her daughter, Jennifer, and how it touched Jennifer's life.

Jennifer was working as a parking lot attendant at the time. One evening a man drove up and asked if he might park in the lot for just ten minutes without paying. Although it was against policy, she gave him permission to do so.

When he left he said to her, "You must get hungry working here," and drove off. A few minutes later he returned with a dinner of curried chicken, rice, and a fortune cookie.

Jennifer was astonished at his kindness and thanked him. They shook hands, and he drove away. Jennifer phoned Barbara to tell her the story and said, "Now I want to do something nice for a total stranger!"

The Bible is full of examples of kindness. The words and actions of Jesus show us the meaning of the word. Kindness is a bit of the unexpected combined with love and creativity. It is a quality that touches others and leaves a lasting impression. Kindness can even change lives. And best of all, it often makes the giver feel as good as the receiver.

Kindness is not a cure for all the ills of this world, but it is certainly a start. In an age of road rage, drive-by shootings, and car jackings, kindness is medicine for the troubled human spirit. It warms your heart and soul.

If you want to win souls for Christ, begin by committing a kindness. It gets a person's attention. Kindness is Christianity in action. It opens the door to the human heart and gives God a chance to enter. Use your imagination and creativity, and then allow God to provide the opportunity.

Kindness is contagious. Start an epidemic.

To make this devotion your own:

• Tell how an act of kindness recently affected your life.
• Talk about why you believe kindness is contagious.
• Give your own definition of kindness.

Life

So if you have been raised with Christ, seek the things that are above, where Christ is, seated at the right hand of God. Set your minds on things that are above, not on things that are on earth, for you have died, and your life is hidden with Christ in God. When Christ who is your life is revealed, then you also will be revealed with him in glory.

(Colossians 3:1-4)

"You have died," Paul says, "and your life is hidden with Christ in God." Think about this for a minute. Do you spend more time thinking about life, or avoiding death? Do you spend more energy thinking that life has the final word, or that death has the final word? According to Paul, life has the final word.

Unfortunately, most of us don't live as though *life* has the final word. Rather, we live as though *death* has the final word. In other words, we don't *live* life, we rather avoid death. Think about the language we use for death. People don't *die* anymore, they pass away. They aren't *dead*, they're just "gone" or are "no longer with us" or are "sleeping." Even at the funeral service we avoid issues of death. It used to be common for the coffin to be lowered into the grave or placed in its resting place with dirt thrown on top of it. But when was the last time you remember the coffin being lowered at a funeral service, let alone dirt thrown on it? Why is that? Is it because we believe life has the final word, or is it rather that we want to avoid death?

"You have died," says Paul, "but have been raised up into a new life with Christ." The challenge as Christians is to refocus our energy from avoiding death to living life. The challenge is to live as though the resurrection makes a difference. The call is to believe that the death of Christ still affects us today. The call is to let God worry about our death, rather than fretting over it ourselves. The call is to let the resurrection free us so that we can help others discover life rather than avoid death.

Satan wants us to focus on death. That is our sin, a sin as old as Adam and Eve. The sin that makes us believe that we can control the destiny of our very lives, that somehow we have the power to save ourselves from death. The idea that we are trying to deal with death in our own, selfish ways, rather than letting God conquer death for us. Or thinking that God has no part in our lives except when we need God. That is sin. That is admitting that death has the final word.

But life has the final word, and God wants us to focus on life. God gives us the ability to focus on life through the resurrection of Jesus, even in the midst of death. Believing in the resurrection frees us to accept death. It acknowledges that even though our lives may be fleeting and even though death may come, it is not the final word. *Life* is the final word.

To make this devotion your own:

- Do you think you spend more time living life or avoiding death? Explain.
- Have you planned any of your funeral arrangements yet? Why or why not?
- What have you learned from others that helps you to "set your mind on things that are above"?

Memories

But remember the LORD your God, for it is he who gives you power to get wealth, so that he may confirm his covenant that he swore to your ancestors, as he is doing today.

(Deuteronomy 8:18)

The old neighborhood may be gone, but the memories still live on. The passing decades have scattered the people, erased the buildings; but people still remember the good old days in the neighborhood where they grew up.

There was Catfish Bob, the homeless guy. His girlfriend was Dirty Gertie. Cool Eye and Sailor Bill were well known in the area as were Greenhorn and Goggles. Primeau's Grocery sold penny grab bags to kids. Other stores down the block included Maurice Lerhner's secondhand clothes, the Silver Dollar Saloon, Kessel's Bakery, and Fannie Breslau's Palace, which burned down when Cigar Butt Louie fell asleep while smoking a cigar. We remember real people and places that now only exist in our memory.

We fondly remember the past when life seemed easier, people were more friendly, the streets were safer, and things were cheaper. We cherish our old friends and neighbors. We remember the stores where we once shopped. And we can't forget the automobiles we drove, which are now classics. We yearn for the past as we live in the present and are nervous about the future.

The good news is that the God who was so good to our ancestors is still with us today. Although times may have changed, our God remains the same. The faith of our fathers and mothers was in a God who was timeless. Their prayers were heard by the same God who still hears our prayers today. The old church may be gone, replaced by an office complex, yet faith still thrives in new congregations across the land. The God we trusted in our childhood is alive and still loves us.

Our God is our past, our present, and our future. God connects us to the saints, the generations who have gone before us. Our grandparents and their parents knew a personal God to whom they turned when things got tough. They may have lived in a world different from ours, but their struggles were much the same. Putting food on the table, making house payments, dealing with illness, tragedy, and death have always been part of life.

So what about our memories? Perhaps God has given us memories to remind us that he is a God of all times. Memories help us see the greatness of God. We remember his kindness, love, and protection just as our parents and grandparents did. The God of the old neighborhood is still with us today.

To make this devotion your own:

• Tell memories of your childhood experiences in learning about God.
• Talk about how your memories strengthen your faith today.
• Tell about the person who shaped your faith in God.

Moving

—=≡≡◎/◎/◎≡≡—

By faith Abraham obeyed when he was called to set out for a place that
he was to receive as an inheritance; and he set out, not knowing where he
was going....If they had been thinking of the land that they had left
behind, they would have had opportunity to return. But as it is, they desire
a better country, that is, a heavenly one. Therefore God is not ashamed to
be called their God; indeed, he has prepared a city for them.
(Hebrews 11:8, 15-16)

Imagine receiving a phone call from someone you hardly know. "I've
got this great place I want you to see," the person begins. "It's a long way
away, but the view is great, and I think you'll like it. You'll have to move
immediately, leave your neighbors and friends and family, and try to learn
a new language along the way since you'll be moving to a foreign country.
And don't worry about a job—I'll try to line one up for you when you
arrive. OK. Any questions? Actually, there's no time for questions—I'll
answer those when you get there. See you soon!"

Chances are Abraham must have felt a little like this when God called
him to leave his familiar surroundings and go to a new land. No specifics,
really, only the promise of a brighter future. "And what did God say about
this?" Sarah must have asked. "And this? And this? And this?"

There are times when God asks us to make moves for which we do not
feel prepared, times when God uproots us from what is safe and familiar
and comfortable to follow him. Times when we do not have
all the answers we want or need. In fact, it may seem like God asks us to
make life-changing decisions with little more than a gut feeling, a sense
of doing something we know we must do. God calls us to act, in faith, and
to trust God to provide for us and to let God take care of the details.

What if Abraham had turned back? What if Abraham had not believed
God's promise? Surely Abraham's homeland must have looked inviting
when new troubles arose enroute to the new land. Surely it would have
been easier to stay with the familiar than to change and uproot and learn
new things. But Abraham continued to look ahead, to look ahead to God's

promise. That is what kept him from turning back. And in the end, that is what allowed him to receive God's promise and inheritance.

What is your first reaction when you feel that God is asking you to move, or when God asks you to do something you're unsure about? Is it to jump forward, or to turn back? Are you tempted to look at things in the past and think they were better than they actually were, using this as an excuse not to move forward? Or do you find yourself putting your trust in the things you can control, rather than leaving the uncontrollable to God?

We will not always have all the answers or information we want when God calls us to move, whether that be to a new homeland, a new neighborhood, a new job, a new family, a new relationship, a new understanding of ourselves, or perhaps even a new faith. No, we will not always have the information we want, but we do have God's promise of protection and care and generosity. Like Abraham, we too will find something better in store if we but trust in God to lead us one step at a time.

To make this devotion your own:

- Tell about a time you moved or did something else "risky" when you did not have all the information you wanted.
- Think of a time you felt like God was asking you or your church to do something you were unsure about. What happened?
- Reflect on ways you've grown in your faith or in your relationship with God by trusting in God when you did not have all the answers.

Mysteries

The King said to Daniel, "Truly, your God is God of gods and Lord of kings and a revealer of mysteries, for you have been able to reveal this mystery!"

(Daniel 2:47)

Jim was a Llewellin Setter owned by a Missouri man named Sam Van Arsdale. Born in 1925, Jim began displaying unbelievable perceptive abilities at the age of three. While on a walk in the woods one day, Van Arsdale discovered his dog possessed humanlike abilities to understand and respond to commands.

The dog could pick out a certain type of tree when requested. He would find an oak or elm tree when asked. Jim could select a specific license plate from a group, or upon entering a home he had never been in before, he could go to a specific room and wait. Jim performed for the Missouri legislature. He was asked in Morse code to go to a specific legislator. Jim promptly went to the right man and put his paw on his leg. The dog also responded to orders given in English, French, German, and Italian.

Sworn affidavits show that Jim predicted the winner of the Kentucky Derby for seven years in a row. Pieces of paper with the names of the horses were placed on the floor, and Jim put his paw on the paper with the name of the winner before the race was run. How did he do it? Only God knows. Jim took all his secrets with him when he died in 1937 at the age of twelve.

Life is certainly full of mysteries, this being one of many. Our knowledge about people, our world, and our universe is limited. We can't even predict the weather with any great degree of accuracy. No one can say why bad things happen to good people or how the pyramids got built. How do miracles happen? What are UFOs? These and many other questions may well forever be mysteries.

God must like mysteries, otherwise he would not have created so many of them. Why don't we know everything? Such information only belongs to God. Mysteries bring us closer to God because we can't and don't know it all. Our understanding as humans is limited because that is how God made us. We can't be God, and we certainly get into trouble when we act like God. Some things just can't be explained and need to be accepted by faith.

As humans, we are often fascinated by the unknown, so perhaps that is why God created mysteries. We can always look to God for answers, and perhaps that is exactly what God intended. God has many secrets, but everything else we need to know can be found in the Bible.

To make this devotion your own:

• Tell about a mystery that gives you a feeling of awe of the power of God.
• Tell why you selected this devotion to read.
• Talk about what mysteries in life you are beginning to understand.

Names

———⟋❀⟋———

So out of the ground the LORD God formed every animal of the field and every bird of the air, and brought them to the man to see what he would call them; and whatever the man called every living creature, that was its name.

(Genesis 2:19)

We live in a world of unusual and fascinating names. Corporations, cities, rivers, and people each have a name, a unique identity that belongs only to them. The name Johnson may be common, but other names may be just plain peculiar. Take the town of Peculiar, Missouri, as an example.

The story goes that a pioneer settler in the area was trying to gain a post office for the town. At the time, the town had no name. The man applied to Washington, D.C., and requested a specific name for his town so he could open a post office. He was told the name he requested was already taken. So he tried again. That name was already taken. Soon, both the man and Washington, D.C., were growing tired of the correspondence and name selection process. Frustrated, the man told Washington, D.C., to select a peculiar name, and that is exactly what happened.

Many names in the Bible are also peculiar. The books of Numbers and Genesis are filled with names of tribes, nations, and people that may seem odd to us. In Genesis, we read about Adam and Eve, Abraham and Sarah, and others who have familiar names. However, the same book also contains the names of such people as Havilah, Ashkenaz, and Sabtecah, names that are difficult to pronounce, much less spell.

To God, names are very important and each has a special meaning. We are told in the Bible that God has named us and knows us by name. Think of it! The God who created the heavens and the universe knows us and calls us by name. We are part of God's creation. From the name on our birth certificate to the name on our grave, the hand of God has an active role because we are God's children.

In Exodus, God reveals his name. God tells Moses in Exodus 3:14 that his name is I AM. Because God wants us to know him and to have a personal relationship with him, God wants us to know his name. We also call God our Father. He is our Lord, our Master, and our Savior Jesus Christ. Throughout the ages, people have called to the name of God for help and salvation.

What's in a name? It is more than identification. It is forever how we are known by others and by God, even if we are a bit peculiar.

To make this devotion your own:

• Share what you think should be considered in selecting a name.
• Talk about why you selected this topic.
• Discuss your view on the importance of a name.

Needs

The LORD is my shepherd,
I shall not want.
(Psalm 23:1)

What are some of the things you want in life? A good marriage? A nice home? How about a happy spouse or happy kids? What about a sense of security in terms of your job, or your finances, or both? How about good health, or a long overdue vacation with your family? Or wouldn't that bright red Mercedes 600 SL you saw the other day be nice? What is it you want out of life?

There's something unnerving about the simplicity of the psalmist when he writes, "The LORD is my shepherd, I shall not want." In the midst of our desires, in the midst of our self-centeredness, in the midst of our worrying about what's going to happen, the Lord says to us, "Don't worry about all the things you want. Rather, let me give you the things you need."

There is a difference between the things we want and the things we actually need. Come to think of it, there's a *big* difference between the things we want and the things we need. We want security. We want love. We want to be cared for. We want to be happy. We want to be fulfilled in our work. And yet, despite the goodness of these things, they all really focus on self. They center on our personal needs, on our own life, on our own situations. Even our desire for a happy spouse and family are really for us—if they're happy, chances are pretty good we'll be happy too. So again the question comes back to confront us—are these simply things we want for our own benefit, or do we really need them?

The psalmist is one smart cookie. He knows that our wants and desires ultimately lead us back to focusing on ourselves. The psalmist, on the other hand, wants us to focus on God. "The LORD is my shepherd, I shall not want." The Lord is the focus. The Lord is the solution, as well. We need not want because God is giving us what we need.

Have you ever wondered why this psalm is so popular at funerals? Sure, it conjures up nice, peaceful images in the midst of death's tumult and chaos. But more important than that is the way it helps us put our focus where it should be—on God, rather than on self. You have to admit, you can feel pretty helpless and even hopeless when you have just lost someone you love. Your nice secure world suddenly goes to pieces in the midst of death. The security you thought you had is gone, despite the work and effort you put in to trying to keep it that way—nice and secure. Death makes things very clear. It weeds out the unimportant. It strips away the unessentials. You don't have to wonder any longer what's important, because you suddenly understand.

God does not always give us what we want, but God does give us what we need. In the midst of our wants we hear the psalmist say, "The LORD is my shepherd, I shall not want." In the midst of an aching heart the psalmist says, "he restores my soul." In the tumultuous rushing of emotions of day-to-day living the psalmist says, "he leads me in right paths." In the frenzy of desperate activity the psalmist says "he makes me lie down in green pastures." The Lord will not always give us what we want, but he will give us what we need. We shall not want because God Almighty is supplying us with our every need. The LORD is our shepherd. And for that reason, we need not want. Not now. Not ever.

To make this devotion your own:

- Think of a time you got something you really wanted. In what ways was it satisfying? In what ways was it not as satisfying as you had hoped?
- What are some things you really want? Which of these things do you really need to survive?
- How does God provide for your needs?

Now!

Besides this, you know what time it is, how it is now the moment for you to wake from sleep. For salvation is nearer to us now than when we became believers; the night is far gone, the day is near.

(Romans 13:11-12)

Have you ever taken that cruise you always thought you'd like to take? How about that ski trip to the mountains? What about that visit to see a special friend, a sick parent, or an aging grandparent? What about that quality time you've anticipated spending with your child? Have you postponed any of the things you've longed to do? If so, what has kept you from enjoying these moments *now*?

Too often we live in the past. We think about what should have taken place or what could have taken place. We relive past events, constantly recycling the same memories over and over again. We should have done this, we should have done that, we think. Or we beat up ourselves for not doing something different, agonizing over every little detail until it keeps us immobile to do something about it now, in the present.

We can also spend too much time thinking and worrying about the future. We focus on what should or could or might happen. Mark Twain once remarked that he had been through some terrible things in his life, some of which actually happened! Time spent worrying about what might happen in the future does nothing for our situation in the present.

The only moment we have is now. The apostle Paul reminds us of this fact as he wraps up his letter to the Romans saying, "Besides this, you know what time it is, how it is now the moment for you to wake from sleep. For salvation is nearer to us now than when we became believers" (Romans 13:11-12). Paul was reminding the people how important it was to live in this world, at this time, in this moment. Past traditions were past. What might happen in the future was not yet determined. The only moment that people had for certain was *now,* and now was the best time to remember and rejoice in God's message of grace and salvation.

Are you living in the *now*? Are you fully awake, fully cognizant of God's love and work in your life now, at this precise moment? Or are you still focusing on past events, past sin, past remembrances that keep you from benefiting from God's present love and forgiveness? As Paul wrote earlier in his letter to the Romans, "God proves his love for us in that while we still were sinners Christ died for us. Much more surely then, now that we have been justified by his blood, will we be saved through him from the wrath of God" (Romans 5:8-9). You don't have to wait until you're a better person to let God love you. You don't have to wait for God to forgive you. God has already taken care of that through Jesus Christ. Here's the truth about the past: it's past! So leave it there. Look to this moment. Look to see how God is working in your life *now*.

How can we focus on the *now*? Focus on God. Focus on God's gift of love, grace, forgiveness, and peace, all given to you for the present moment. Take time now, this moment, to listen for what God is saying to you. How does God want to be involved in your life at this time? Or meditate on a verse of Scripture. Think of how it speaks to you now, what the verse is saying to you, and what you can learn from it. As the old saying goes, there is no time like the present, especially when that present moment includes God.

To make this devotion your own:

• Think of ways you live in the past, or ways you live thinking about the future.
• Tell about a time you were anxious about the future. What happened? Did the event ever take place?
• Reflect on ways you can live *now,* in the present.

Opportunity

Therefore, as we have opportunity, let us do good to all people, especially to those who belong to the family of believers.

(Galatians 6:10 NIV)

The story is told of a farmer who sold his farm to go in search of diamonds. The man traveled all over the world and ended up broke and depressed. He eventually drowned himself in a river because his treasure had eluded him.

This tale did not end with the man's death, however. It seems that the man who purchased the farm was watering his livestock one day and discovered a glistening object in the stream. It was a diamond! His discovery led to virtually "acres of diamonds" on his property.

You may have heard this "acres of diamonds" story before, but have you ever considered the message it has for Christians? How often do we overlook the obvious? The grass always looks greener somewhere else. We often search and search for something that is right under our nose. We overlook the opportunity in our own backyard!

Christianity does begin at home. There is no need to travel far away. Mission can begin with your family, a neighbor, or the guy who rides the bus with you. Service to others does not necessarily mean a trip to Africa. It can start at a shelter for the homeless in your community or by visiting those in a hospital. Nursing homes and jails are also local sources of outreach.

Your own church can contain "acres of diamonds." Involvement in youth ministry, food drives, choir, committees, Sunday school, ushering, and even property maintenance can give you an opportunity to give glory to God. God does work in strange ways and in the most common places. You don't have to go far to find a person in need.

God calls you to serve right where you are. Open your eyes. Acres of diamonds are closer than you think!

To make this devotion your own:

- Tell of some local opportunities for Christian service that are overlooked.
- Share how you discovered "diamonds" right under your nose.
- Begin this devotion by holding up a fake or real diamond and saying where you discovered it.

Opportunity

Be wise in the way you act toward outsiders, make the most of every opportunity.

(Colossians 4:5 NIV)

About two thousand years ago, a man missed an opportunity to have his name and kindness remembered forever.

You know the story well. The man operated a small inn in the town of Bethlehem. One evening two weary travelers came to his inn, a young man and a woman who was about to give birth. They needed a place to stay, but for one reason or another he turned them away. Perhaps he was saving his last room for someone who could pay him more. Or maybe he didn't even have time to talk with the couple and told a helper to get rid of them.

Today the man and his inn are unknown because he missed the opportunity to be a part of the greatest story ever told. Joseph and Mary located a stable, and it is there that Jesus was born.

The Bible also tells of people who accepted opportunities from God. Noah built an ark. The disciples followed Christ. And countless individuals were healed by Jesus because they took the opportunity to come to him.

God gives us opportunities every day. Like the owner of the inn, we may not recognize an opportunity when we see it. Opportunities don't come with bells and whistles; they come in the form of people, problems, and situations where help is needed.

An opportunity will certainly come your way soon. It may be today, tomorrow, or next week. Keep your eyes and ears open. Pray that you may recognize God's call to service. There may have been no room for Joseph and Mary at the inn, but 2000 years later God may be asking you to make room in your life for someone who needs your help.

To make this devotion your own:

• Talk about an opportunity that got away from you.
• Discuss an opportunity you accepted and tell why you did it.
• Talk about an opportunity you are searching for and why.

Outlook

Let each of you look not to your own interests, but to the interests of others. Let the same mind be in you that was in Christ Jesus.

(Philippians 2:4-5)

There once was a little girl who found a dime on the sidewalk. She was so thrilled with her discovery that she got into the habit of looking down on the ground for coins wherever she went. She found many pennies, nickels, dimes, and even quarters, and kept them all in a jar at home. It was exciting because she never knew what she would find next; and best of all, it was free!

Years went by and her downward search continued. The total of money grew and grew. Her treasure could be measured in dollars as decades passed. She also found a ring and a watch, but sadly she never knew what she missed. By looking down the woman missed many a sunset, beautiful birds in the trees, children flying kites and carrying balloons, magnificent buildings and statues, the splendor of tall mountains, and fascinating cloud formations.

It is sad that some people miss the best that life has to offer because they focus on the unimportant. They look at the faults of others and at their own aches and pains, and worry about things that may never happen. They find what they seek. Often they find the pennies on the ground, but they miss the treasure that is theirs for the taking just because they look in the wrong direction.

God offers the abundant life. It is free for the asking and begins with our outlook. If we look to God, we are given all we need. God provides us with food, clothing, health, work, friends, and family. We need to look no further to find the peace, happiness, and love we seek in life. God's blessings come with no strings attached, and we don't even have to look for them.

The choice is ours. We can look to God and be blessed. We can look down at the dirt or into a beautiful blue sky. We can see the good in others, or we can just look for the bad. Our attitude and outlook determine so much in life.

President Abraham Lincoln said it best. "Most people are about as happy as they make up their minds to be."

To make this devotion your own:

• Tell the experience that taught you the importance of a positive attitude.
• Talk about the connection between your spiritual life and your happiness.
• Discuss how you have been blessed by God.

Payoff

*O give thanks to the L*ORD*, for he is good,*
for his steadfast love endures forever.

It is he who remembered us in our low estate,
for his steadfast love endures forever;
and rescued us from our foes,
for his steadfast love endures forever;
who gives food to all flesh,
for his steadfast love endures forever.

O give thanks to the God of heaven,
for his steadfast love endures forever.
(Psalm 136:1, 23-26)

Willie Sutton, a notorious bank robber, was asked by a reporter why he robbed banks. "Because that's where the money is," he replied. His response was dubbed "Sutton's Law."

While Willie's remark may seem rather obvious at first, it is really quite profound. Willie put his time and energy and effort where he knew there was going to be a payoff. Rather than spending time on grocery stores or insurance buildings or veterinarian clinics, he focused on banks. That's where the money was. And that's where Willie focused his time and energy.

Like Willie Sutton, the psalmist knew where his payoff was. His wealth, his hope, his prosperity, his very life depended on God. Each of the twenty-six verses in this psalm ends exactly the same way: "for his steadfast love endures forever." The psalmist had no doubt what was important in life. He focused on God because that's where the payoff was. He prayed, he worshiped, he gave thanks to God because God was the one who provided for his every need. It was not Baal or the sun or the moon or his children or his spouse who rescued him and steadfastly loved him. It was God, the God of Abraham and Sarah and Ruth and Jacob.

Where do you find your payoff? On what do you spend your time and energy? What is it that preoccupies your thoughts throughout the day? On what do you rely when you need to cash in? If someone were to rob your heart, what would they find in the hidden recesses?

Funny, isn't it? If God is the payoff, if God is the real prize, if God is the source of real wealth and happiness, if our very lives depend on God, why don't we spend more time with God? If God is the answer, why do we waste so much of our time elsewhere? Why do we look for happiness in jobs, or in paychecks, or in relationships, or in keeping busy, or in trying to be religious? If the real payoff is in God, why don't we spend every minute, every hour, every day of our lives focusing on God? God is the one who will always be there. God is the one who will always love us. God, and only God, has the steadfast love that endures forever.

To make this devotion your own:

• Recall a time when God's steadfast love was real to you.
• Tell what the term "steadfast love" means to you.
• Share ways in which you feel God's steadfast love is reflected in your church, family, or neighborhood.

Prayer

If you believe, you will receive whatever you ask for in prayer.
(Matthew 21:22 NIV)

It didn't look like the answer to a prayer. The huge, yellow 1978 Mercury Monarch had seen better days. It had dents, some rust, and was slightly out of alignment; yet it was the most beautiful car in the world to the new owner.

Hours earlier, a young man with no money and in great need of a car, prayed to God for help. Now, a friend of a friend, someone he didn't even know, was giving him the keys and title to a working automobile, all at no cost. The giver had an extra car he didn't need, and the recipient was left speechless by the generosity of a stranger, and by the power of prayer.

The car, which had a fatal defect in the engine, lasted exactly one year before it died one afternoon in a grocery store parking lot. The Monarch had been virtually maintenance-free during that period of time. And now the owner had saved enough money to buy another car.

Prayers do not always receive such a quick and positive response, but answered prayers are the ones we tend to remember and convey to others. Sometimes we pray and wonder if God even hears us. We pray and wait for an answer to our requests and concerns. And often it seems that patience and persistence are the two essential elements in our daily prayer life.

Anyone who has prayed knows our prayers are not always answered immediately. And often we may not get the answers we want. God answers prayer in his own ways and on his own timetable, according to his plans. God knows what is best for us. We need to remember that.

Yet there is something more to prayer. It is more than asking and waiting. Prayer is a gift. It is the ability, given to us by God, to communicate with him. Our God, the creator of all, listens to us. He could have put us on earth to live out our lives and deal with problems alone, but our loving God instead established prayer as an eternal link with him. Prayer is a twenty-four-hour-a-day lifeline where we can go to get answers and an eager listener. Prayer is the most powerful source on earth, and it is a gift to us from God.

It has been said that prayer is like a key that opens a door. It is more than that. It is a key to a conversation with God.

To make this devotion your own:

• Share some of your experiences with prayer.
• Begin or end this devotion with your own prayer.
• Talk about answered versus unanswered prayer.

Protection

For it is the Lord our God who brought us and our ancestors up from the land of Egypt....He protected us along all the way that we went.

(Joshua 24:17)

The story is told of a bird that was looking for a spot to build her nest. She found a wonderful location high in a tree. It had an excellent view. Then a hawk flew by, and the bird realized it was not a safe place to build a home.

The bird then discovered a beautiful field with green grass and flowers. This would be the perfect place for a nest, she thought. Then a cat approached and the bird fled the green field.

Finally the bird landed near a thorn bush. It wasn't pretty and didn't offer much of a view, but at least it was safe. The thorns would protect the mother and her babies. Time passed and her babies were born. And bright red roses appeared among the thorns, so now the bird had a home that was not only safe but also beautiful. She realized the thorns were actually a blessing, and the bird praised God for her protection. (Adapted from *On Our Father's Knee*, Fredrik Wisløff [Oslo, Norway: Nordstrand Books, 1964], pp. 67-68)

We often don't see the hand of God protecting us. We sometimes see it after the fact, when we have escaped from danger. An illness caught in the nick of time, a near miss in a car accident, a robbery or burglary that is thwarted reminds us of the goodness of God. We are lucky. We are fortunate. We are blessed by a God who protects us.

The thorns in our life can also be a blessing. Troubles change us. They challenge us and make us stronger. We can sometimes look back at what we thought were the worst years and see how they guided us to a better place. And we see it wasn't an accident that things turned out the way they did. We see the protecting hand of God.

Life offers no guarantees. We are given life moment by moment, but we are not promised a tomorrow. Life can take a sudden turn for the worse. That's when we turn to God for protection. We are never closer to God than in times when we need him the most.

George McDonald has a keen insight about how God protects us. He says, "How often we look upon God as our last and feeblest resource! We go to him because we have nowhere else to go. And then we learn that the storms of life have driven us, not upon the rocks, but into the desired haven."

To make this devotion your own:

• Tell about a time in your life when you felt God's protection.
• Talk about a struggle or problem that actually was a blessing for you.
• Tell the group why you selected this devotion to share.

Rebellion

Yet they tested the Most High God,
and rebelled against him.
They did not observe his decrees.
    (Psalm 78:56)

Jet, a black cocker spaniel, often has an ear infection. He rubs his ear on the floor or against one of his bones to ease the irritation. It is then that his master brings out the eardrops, and Jet launches a full-scale rebellion. First, Jet will run and hide if he spots the tube of medicine. When captured, Jet will shake his head from side to side making it impossible to get the drops near his ear. When all else fails, he will lie on his back with all four feet in the air, again moving his head and ears away from the tube. The outcome is always the same. Jet eventually loses the battle as his master does what is best for him. Jet has yet to learn the master always wins. And despite his rebellious ways, his master loves him.

The Bible is filled with stories of rebellion. Slaves rebel against masters. Nations rebel against nations. Sons rebel against their fathers. The Bible is a book that details rebellion against God. It is a history of people trying to resist God. From the book of Genesis to the book of Revelation, humans try to escape the will of God. It's an ongoing battle as old as time.

Why do we rebel? It is a battle of wills. The will of God is based on love and knowing what is best for us. Our will leads us to believe that we know what is best for us and that we can successfully escape from God and his love. Sin leads us to question God's authority. We know God's will, yet we give in to our own desires. Rebellion begins when we fool ourselves into believing the big lie.

The cost of this rebellion is separation from God. Although we never lose God's love for us, our personal relationship suffers. As much as we try to deny it, we know something is not right. Perhaps we struggle and go along without God for a while, but in the end we come back to God through prayer and repentance. And God forgives us, restores us, and continues to love us. Rebellion is never the answer. Surrender is a much better strategy.

God knows best. God has our best interests at heart, loves us more than we know, and wants to have a personal relationship with us. That's a cause for celebration, not rebellion.

To make this devotion your own:

• Talk about a time you rebelled against God and what happened.
• Share your thoughts about rebellion in today's society.
• Tell why you chose this devotion to read.

Rubble

=@@@=

How long, O LORD? Will you forget me forever?
How long will you hide your face from me?
How long must I bear pain in my soul,
and have sorrow in my heart all day long?

But I trusted in your steadfast love;
my heart shall rejoice in your salvation.
I will sing to the LORD,
because he has dealt bountifully with me.
(Psalm 13:1-2, 5-6)

In 1989 a massive earthquake rocked Europe and crushed an entire village. In less than ten minutes 30,000 people died.

There was a father in the village who walked his son to school every single day. And every single day he told his son, "Armond, I will always be here for you. No matter what happens, I will always be here for you."

The earthquake struck when the father had returned home from walking his son to school. He and his wife survived the initial impact of the quake, but terror struck his heart as he thought about his son at school. He raced back to the place where he had just left Armond minutes before. The school was leveled. Nearby gas leaks and explosions shook the ground as this father could only think the worst. What had happened to Armond?

The father went to the part of the school where he usually picked up his son and began to dig furiously amidst the rubble and fire. A policeman came by and told him he had to leave for safety reasons. "Are you going to help me?" was the father's only response. Six hours later a fireman told the father the same thing, for explosions still rocked the village in the aftermath of the earthquake. "Are you going to help me?" the father asked for the second time. Hours passed, and parents of other school children came to the scene, dazed and terror stricken. They cried and yelled for their sons and daughters but heard nothing. Nor did they help. As people walked away from the debris, they could see Armond's father still digging, sixteen hours after the quake. Twenty-four hours passed, then thirty hours. Armond's father was still digging despite his fatigue and numbness and bloody hands. People implored him to leave for his own safety, but still he refused. Thirty-six hours, and he was still digging. He pulled another rock off the pile and heard a voice say, "Dad? Dad, is that you?"

"Armond, Armond!" the father cried.

"Dad, I knew you'd come back for me. I knew you'd be here, just like you said."

"Armond, are you alone?"

"No Dad, there are fifteen other kids here with me. We huddled against a wall in the basement when the building started shaking. We're OK, but we're scared and hungry."

"Armond, grab my hand so that I can pull you out."

"No, Dad. Help the other kids first. I know you'll always be here for me."

Though there are times when God seems to be very far away, sometimes God is the only one digging, like this father, to help us survive. When our lives are in pain and in rubble and we are numb because of what's happening all around us, God is there fighting, struggling, and bleeding for us so that we might live. Death and destruction may be looking us in the face, but God is there to love and guide us. Though everything else may collapse, though everyone around us may leave, God is there for us, especially in the midst of the rubble.

To make this devotion your own:

- Tell about a time you felt like things were crumbling all around you. How did your faith help?
- Think of a time you waited and prayed for God to help you. What happened?
- Compare how God is like Armond's father who keeps digging in the rubble until he finds and saves us.

Safety

You are our LORD and our God! We ask you to keep us safe.
(Isaiah 37:20 CEV)

The Assyrian army was a war machine. The earth literally shook when its vast army and cavalry lined up to attack. It had chewed up and spit out powerful nations. One by one, kingdom after kingdom fell. The small remnant of God's people in Judah could feel the hot breath of this nightmare as the Assyrian army advanced with little resistance. The king of Assyria sent this message to Hezekiah, the king of Judah.

Don't trust your God or be fooled by his promise to defend Jerusalem against me. You have heard how we Assyrian kings have completely wiped out other nations. What makes you feel so safe? The Assyrian kings before me destroyed the towns of Gozan, Haran, Rezeph, and everyone from Eden who lived in Telassar. What good did their gods do them? The kings of Hamath, Arpad, Sepharvaim, Hena, and Ivvah have all disappeared. (Isaiah 37:10-13 CEV)

After reading this note from the king of Assyria, Hezekiah "took it to the temple and spread it out for the Lord to see." He then prayed:

It is true, our LORD, that Assyrian kings have turned nations into deserts. They destroyed the idols of wood and stone that the people of those nations had made and worshiped. But you are our LORD and our God! We ask you to keep us safe from the Assyrian king. Then everyone in every kingdom on earth will know that you are the only LORD." (Isaiah 37:18-20 CEV)

Assyria did not attack Judah. The Lord sent an angel to the Assyrian camp and killed 185,000 of them all in one night. Sennacherib, king of Assyria, returned to his city of Nineveh, where he was killed by his two sons while worshiping his god Nisroch.

Miraculous, don't you think? Who would have ever bet against such odds? In the same situation would you have staked your life on God like Hezekiah did?

No doubt we have run before much smaller enemies than the death-machine of the Assyrian army. Unpaid bills take on a monstrous life of their own. Upcoming work deadlines loom dark on the horizon, belching black smoke and chanting, "I dare you." Day-to-day responsibilities gang up to form huge alliances that threaten to disarm us, piece by piece. Forget the threat of death—the minor struggles of a new day can often be enough to send us running for cover.

Hezekiah reminds us that God is someone we can turn to when life seems overwhelming. God is a God of safety. God is our net of protection, our blanket of security, our giver of life in the midst of death. And yet we need not wait until things become desperate to turn to God. God yearns to forgive us. God waits to help us. God wants to be with us now. God longs to love us today, this moment.

Let God help you today. Move over and let God be your partner. Like Hezekiah, spread out your joys, your sorrows, your needs, and your thanks before God. Let God be your army. Let God be your guide. Let God be your strength and comforter. Let God be God so that you can be the person God wants you to be—a person who can do remarkable things with God.

To make this devotion your own:

• Recall a time as a child when you felt very safe.
• Think of a time you hesitated to ask God for help.
• Tell about a time God protected you from an "enemy."

Shadows

Yea, though I walk through the valley of the shadow of death, I will fear no evil: for thou art with me; thy rod and thy staff they comfort me.

(Psalm 23:4 KJV)

You could peer over the steep edge if you were careful of the loose limestone that made sure footing precarious at best. The cliffs dropped suddenly and sharply, like a mini Grand Canyon in the middle of Israel. A small river several hundred feet below cut through the limestone, forming a valley with steep cliffs on both sides. If you listened carefully you could hear the running water, but it was too dark and too far down to actually see water. A few patches of green, evidences of moisture in the otherwise barren land, broke up the browns and yellows of the high limestone walls. It wasn't even noon yet, but much of the valley below was in dark shadows. In fact, much of the valley remained in shadows throughout the day. The narrow chasm was a miser in terms of exposing the valley below to light.

If you looked hard at the other side of the limestone wall you could see the dotted foot path winding through the valley below. Those who dared to walk this path were at the mercy of deadly wild animals or bandits that inhabited this place. This dangerous parcel of wilderness was on the ancient road from Jerusalem to Jericho. Remember the parable of the good Samaritan, Jesus' story in Luke 10 about a man going down from Jerusalem to Jericho who fell into the hands of robbers and was stripped, beaten, and left for dead? This was the "valley of the shadow of death."

Those familiar with Psalm 23 and the allusion to the valley of the shadow of death need no interpretation from this lofty vantage point. The meaning of the psalm becomes instantly clear. One look into the chasm below and you could understand the feelings of dread sojourners must have felt two and three thousand years ago. Even the thoughts of seasoned travelers must have been to make it through that dangerous valley as quickly as possible, to get beyond the darkness and the cold and the threat of death.

In what valleys or shadows have you sojourned lately? When have you felt the dread of an upcoming journey, appointment, presentation, or meeting with someone? When have you felt threatened, or insecure, because of the circumstances surrounding you?

God is our shepherd, our guardian, our protector. Though we may feel engulfed by all the shadows the world can dish up, the enduring light and presence of God shines forth to give us hope and light and safety. God's presence illumines our paths so that we might face the dangers of struggles of the day and remain victorious with God. God is with us. The great shepherd comes anew to us each day by the power of the Spirit, guiding us and keeping us safe. God will never leave us nor forsake us, no matter how lonely or vulnerable we may feel. For "yea, though I walk through the valley of the shadow of death, I will fear no evil: for thou art with me; thy rod and thy staff they comfort me" (Psalm 23:4 KJV).

To make this devotion your own:

- Recall a time when you felt like you were walking through the "valley of the shadow of death."
- Think of a time God comforted you and gave you peace in the midst of a difficult time.
- Share ways that God is your shepherd, someone who nurtures you and cares for you.

Strength

Therefore, to keep me from being too elated, a thorn was given me in the flesh, a messenger of Satan to torment me, to keep me from being too elated. Three times I appealed to the Lord about this, that it would leave me, but he said to me, "My grace is sufficient for you, for power is made perfect in weakness." So, I will boast all the more gladly of my weaknesses, so that the power of Christ may dwell in me. Therefore I am content with weaknesses, insults, hardships, persecutions, and calamities for the sake of Christ; for whenever I am weak, then I am strong.

(2 Corinthians 12:7-10)

It came out of nowhere. In fact, the father didn't have a clue why his six-year-old son had even asked the question. "Dad, you're really strong, aren't you?" And even though the father figured that only part of the question had to do with actual physical strength, he knew it was important to his son that he could say yes, at least in part.

Perhaps it's a guy thing—being strong and all. It ties into the male identity. It defines, at least in part, who men are. It questions whether men have what it takes to make it in this world of do-it-yourselfers. And it's not just a surface issue like the I-bet-my-Dad-can-beat-up-your-Dad variety. It's about who we are as people. It is about whether or not we are really complete if we admit our weaknesses.

Weakness is not something we brag about. It's not something we strive for. It's not a compliment when someone says, "Boy, you're really weak." No, we want strength. It's an advantage to be strong, physically and mentally. But that, precisely, is our weakness, our downfall.

Notice that God did not take away the "thorn in the flesh" the apostle Paul talked about. God used it as a way for Paul to focus on God's strength. It's OK to revel in our strength if that strength comes from God, otherwise it's simply another tool that keeps us from God.

In what ways are you strong? What can you do by yourself? In what areas do you pride yourself in being self-sufficient? These are the areas where thorns may be found; thorns that keep us away from God.

Rejoice in your weakness. Rejoice when you suddenly discover that the situation is too big for you to handle by yourself. Rejoice when you feel overwhelmed by your own doing. For it is in these situations that you discover your need for God. It is in these situations that you discover how little you need yourself and how much you need God. It is in these situations where you can rest in the strength of God's loving arms. It is in these situations that you can say with the apostle Paul, "whenever I am weak, then I am strong."

To make this devotion your own:

• Think of modern day "thorns in the flesh," things that keep us away from God.

• Tell a time when God's strength was able to work through your weakness.

• Reflect on what this means for you in terms of your faith: "whenever I am weak, then I am strong."

Stubbornness

So the heart of Pharaoh was hardened, and he would not let the Israelites go, just as the LORD had spoken through Moses.

(Exodus 9:35)

Frogs. Grasshoppers. Hail. Darkness. Boils. Flies. Maggots. Blood. Death. What would it take to turn your heart back to God? Some say Pharaoh was stubborn. Some say Pharaoh was proud. Others say Pharaoh was simply God's puppet. Still others say Pharaoh was just plain stupid. Whatever the case, it's hard to be very sympathetic with Pharaoh. Time after time Moses gave Pharaoh a chance to avoid disaster. Time after time Pharaoh refused to let the Israelites go worship God. That is, until the pain was great enough. Then Pharaoh promised to grant Moses' request if Moses could get God to stop the onslaught of each plague. Sure enough, each plague stopped. Sure enough, Pharaoh suddenly changed his mind. And who paid for Pharaoh's stubbornness? The people of Egypt. Yes, Pharaoh suffered, but he did not suffer alone. It was the nation of Egypt that felt the fury of God's wrath when Pharaoh refused, time after time, to let Moses and the Israelites go to worship God.

This story might not seem to be about us, at least at first. It is about a proud king thousands of years ago who is simply trying to protect his property. He wants to hang on to his investments, his power, his boundaries, his gods. But the harder he holds on, the greater the destruction. The more he focuses on his own interests, the more he loses in the process. At first it is only an inconvenience, but in the end the result is death.

How would you have responded if you had been Pharaoh, king of Egypt? Would you have acted any differently?

Think about your own life for a minute. What kingdoms have you ruled throughout your lifetime? What people have been affected by your decisions? How often have you clung stubbornly to certain issues, decisions, or actions until the pain was so great you were forced to change your mind? Yes, we are all Pharaohs who want to protect our people, our children, our family, our investments. There are times when we are all

Pharaohs who stand up against God, even if we know it is wrong. We are all Pharaohs who reluctantly admit, when the pain is great enough, that God is right and we are wrong.

God doesn't want our pain. God wants our hearts. God wants hearts that can be filled with love and hope and peace. God wants hearts that welcome the Spirit in peace rather than hearts that fight against it as an enemy threat. God wants you, plain and simple. And God will go to great lengths to show just how much God wants you.

So the next time you have an inkling to exert your power or to stubbornly remain opposed to what you know God wants you to do, try to avoid it—like the plague. And see what miracles God can do.

To make this devotion your own:

• Would you say you are more like Pharaoh or more like Moses? Explain.
• Share a few small ways that you resist doing what God wants you to do.
• Reflect on some of the consequences in your own life of following, or not following, God.

Synergism

Therefore I am content with weaknesses, insults, hardships, persecutions, and calamities for the sake of Christ; for whenever I am weak, then I am strong.

(2 Corinthians 12:10)

In ancient Greek literature there is a story that shows the power of working together, or synergism. "An aged, dying father called his seven sons around him. He gave each one a stick and told them to break it. Each son easily broke his separate stick. The old father then bound seven sticks and gave the bundle to his eldest son and told him to break the bundle. The eldest son could not do it. Then the second son was commanded to try. He could not. Nor could any of the rest.

"So is it to be of you," said the father. "Alone you are weak, together you are strong."

Synergism is derived from the Greek word "synergos" meaning "working together." It means that by joining with others, common objectives can be more easily accomplished. There is strength in numbers when you multiply your efforts through others.

The Christian church works best when it works together. The mission of proclaiming the gospel to all the nations has greater effectiveness when Christians, congregations, and denominations join hands in a common effort. Using the power of synergism, the poor, the homeless, the ill, and the hungry can be helped and can learn about the love of Jesus.

Synergism also combines the talents of individuals. Christians who have computer skills are teamed with those who have gifts in teaching or public speaking. Pastors can be teamed with laypeople. Those who have a talent for music can be used in a group effort in a presentation of the gospel. People working together are not only more effective, they can reach a goal faster and more cost effectively. Working together means pooling our talent, money, and resources toward one common goal.

Synergism does not mean people have to be alike, think alike, or believe the same things. Synergism does mean that people are willing to work side by side, respect one another, and combine their talents and energy.

How does synergism begin? It starts when you as an individual or group volunteer to help another individual or group. Alone we are weak. Together we are strong and can spread the gospel.

To make this devotion your own:

• Share a goal that you believe can be accomplished by working together.
• Discuss how synergism has worked successfully in the past.
• Present a visual message to the group using a single stick and a bundle of sticks.

Time

===*o/o/o*===

After Jesus had spoken these words, he looked up to heaven and said, "Father, the hour has come; glorify your Son so that the Son may glorify you." (*John 17:1*)

On an episode of the television series *Touched by an Angel,* one of the angels is observing people rushing about, trying not to run out of time. She remarks how foolish people are because they don't realize how infinite time is and that in reality, all we have is time.

Time is misunderstood by many people. We talk about "saving time" and "managing time" when in fact, time cannot be saved or managed. Time cannot be saved and put in a box to be used at a later date, nor can it be managed. Time is only a way of measuring life. It can't be wasted, saved, used, or spent. Life can be wasted, but time cannot.

It's been said that to blame time for your lack of accomplishment or for being tardy is like blaming a thermometer for the heat. Time only tells you how you use the precious hours and days that God has given you. Lack of time does not limit your income, nor does it prevent you from accomplishing your dreams. A wise man once said the secret to life is scheduling your priorities instead of your time.

God gives us life, measured by minutes, hours, days, weeks, months, and years. It is a free gift without restrictions. God goes even further, however. He offers us the promise of eternal life, or time without end. Time is a commodity we cannot purchase, nor can we purchase life. That is what makes both time and life so valuable. When it comes to life, we need to remember what is valuable and what is not.

So how do we make the most of this precious gift? We might begin by focusing on why God gives us time in the first place. God wants us to focus on him, to grow spiritually, and to serve as God's hands and voice in this world. To fill your day with priorities makes the best use of time. We do need to sleep, eat, and work, but family, friends, and God also need to be included in our daily plan. Time and life work out best when we achieve a balance in our activities.

Time is a measurement of our past, present, and future. It was here before we existed and will be here long after we are gone from this earth. In the words of Henry David Thoreau, "Time is but the stream I go a-fishing in." It is also God's most valuable gift to you.

To make this devotion your own:

- Share some of your personal observations about time.
- Tell your own priorities when it comes to time.
- Use a clock, watch, or timer—or all three—as a visual focus for this devotion.

Tuned In

—⟋⟍⟋⟍⟋—

For those who live according to the flesh set their minds on the things of the flesh, but those who live according to the Spirit set their minds on the things of the Spirit. To set the mind on the flesh is death, but to set the mind on the Spirit is life and peace.

(Romans 8:5-6)

No doubt you've had this experience yourself. You're driving in the car or going on a trip, listening to your favorite tunes, beboppin' and singing to the music, when suddenly tragedy strikes. You suddenly go out of range of your favorite radio station. The music stops. Depression sets in. "Now what am I going to do?" you wonder aloud. "This isn't going to be any fun now. It's just static."

What had once been fun isn't fun any longer. What had made the journey more enjoyable had ended. What had made the difference between a good time and a boring time had just quit—it was just more enjoyable when you could listen to your favorite radio station.

It's an inevitable question that always surfaces when people are discussing prayer. It goes something like this: If God knows what we need even before we ask, why ask? Why ask God for something in prayer that God would give us anyway? Since God knows all our needs, why do we have to be involved in the process by praying?

Perhaps we need to look at the question a little differently. Perhaps we need to think about it in terms of our favorite radio station. Could it be that God answers our prayer and we just don't hear it? Could it be that God works in our lives and we just don't see it because we're not on the same frequency as God? Could it be that when we pray for something, we start tuning into God more closely, looking for the ways God is going to work? Like buying a blue minivan and suddenly noticing that six other people on our block have the exact same minivan, could it be that when we set our minds on God we start seeing things we hadn't seen before? Could it be we start seeing God more closely and more often? Could it be possible that God has been answering our prayers all along and we just haven't noticed it? What if the issue isn't whether God answers prayer, but whether we have been tuned in to God? What if the answer is not how much God loves us but how often we take notice of God's love?

Are you and God on the same wavelength? Are you tuned in to the same frequency? Are you hearing the messages God wants you to hear, or have you missed all the love songs, all the serenades, all the passionate choruses and refrains because you haven't been listening? Or have you simply tuned God out? Have you shut off your connection with God because you've put so much distance between you and God that you begin to hear static?

"To set the mind on the flesh is death, but to set the mind on the Spirit is life and peace," writes the apostle Paul. Like listening to your favorite radio station, it's just a lot more fun and enjoyable if you are tuned in to God at the right frequency and can hear all the messages God sends you throughout the day.

How does your faith radio sound these days? Are you listening at the right frequencies? And how are you doing as a receiver? Life can be clearer and more purposeful as we tune ourselves in to the life and love of our Maker.

To make this devotion your own:

• Think about your favorite radio station. Why do you like listening to it?
• Recount someone in your own life who was in tune with God. What did this person do? How did he or she act?
• Tell ways you are able to tune in to God, to set your mind on the things of the Spirit.

Usefulness

—⟨∞∞⟩—

You are the salt of the earth; but if salt has lost its taste, how can its saltiness be restored? It is no longer good for anything, but is thrown out and trampled under foot. (Matthew 5:13)

Porcupines and people tend to stay away from each other. Like most wild animals, porcupines are afraid of humans and try to keep their distance. That's fine with most people who fear being the target of the quills of an angry porcupine.

There is something, however, that can draw the reclusive porcupine toward civilization—salt. Porcupines crave salt and have been known to gnaw almost anything to get it, including glass containers and even wooden handles containing dried perspiration. Salt is highly valued by the porcupine.

In Jesus' day, salt was also quite valuable. That's one reason he used it in an illustration about being valued as a person. Salt had three unique qualities that made it special to people. It represented purity, acted as a preservative, and added flavor. It's those same three qualities that Jesus sees as defining the life and actions of a Christian.

Today when a person is called "the salt of the earth," it is a high compliment because it means that person is valued and useful. People who possess the qualities of salt are treasured because of what they add to life and to their relationships with others. These people are unusual because of their beliefs and values.

Jesus wants his followers to have the properties of salt in their words and deeds. Just as salt is known for purity, Jesus wants Christians to be examples of purity. We need to be reflections of Jesus in what we say and what we do. Salt, which is pure and glistening, represents one standard for the Christian.

Salt is also a preservative. That's another quality for Christians to strive for in daily life. Christians need to add freshness to life and to their relationships. Just as salt acts as a preservative and prevents decay, Christians can help keep situations and people from going bad by preserving the good in life.

Finally, salt adds flavor. As Christians, we can add flavor to life. Jesus wants his followers to add spice to situations and relationships. Our values allow us to see things differently. Our zest can be contagious. We can make the world a better place as we act and speak on Christ's behalf.

If salt loses its properties, Jesus points out, it is no longer good for anything. That's the way it is for us also. We need to be useful and to serve a purpose. Whether it is in giving, loving, teaching, helping, praying, or caring, we serve God and his purpose. Anything less has no value. God calls us to be useful. In doing so, we can be as one of millions of grains of salt, adding freshness, purity, and flavor to life.

To make this devotion your own:

• Discuss a time or incident in your life that made you feel useful.
• Talk about specific ways people can be more useful in your community or in your church.
• Discuss the costs of being useful. What price have you paid?

Viewpoint

—⟨⟩⟨⟩⟨⟩—

We live by faith, not by sight.
(2 Corinthians 5:7 NIV)

There was a movie listing in the newspaper recently that described a classic film. It read, "Transported to a surreal landscape, a young girl accidentally kills the first woman she meets, then teams up with three complete strangers to kill the woman's sister for personal gain."
Sound familiar? It is a description for *The Wizard of Oz,* one of the most beloved films of all time. The synopsis of the movie is technically correct, but it certainly comes from an unusual viewpoint. Actually, this description of *The Wizard of Oz* could have been written in many ways. The viewpoint of the Wicked Witch would certainly be different from that of the Scarecrow. And if you ask any two people about this movie, chances are you could get two completely different answers. It all depends on your viewpoint.

What about God's viewpoint? How does God see us? The Bible provides many answers. He sees us as his children. We are sinners in need of redemption, and that is why Jesus came to our world. John 3:16 tells us "For God so loved the world that he gave his only Son, so that everyone who believes in him may not perish but may have eternal life." As children of God, we have unlimited potential. And that is how God sees us because God loves us so much.

So how should we view others as children of God? We have been given the Ten Commandments to live by. These rules guide our actions toward one another. The Bible tells us we need to love others as God has loved us. We should view ourselves as servants of God, his hands and feet in this world. Our viewpoint should be one of compassion to the poor, the sick, the hungry, and those in prison. And most important, as children of God we can view everyone as relatives because we are brothers and sisters in Christ!

Viewpoints do differ. Lutherans, United Methodists, Presbyterians, and other denominations all have different views about God and worship, yet all worship the same God. The many denominations in this world are an illustration of how diverse our viewpoints can be and what they can do.

Viewpoints can separate us from each other and from our God. Love unites us.

How we see ourselves and how we see others is an important aspect of living the Christian life. We are God's children, and so are the people around us. Think about your views. Are they helping or hindering the kingdom of God?

To make this devotion your own:

• Share how some of your views have changed over the years.
• Discuss some of your strongest views about living as a Christian.
• Talk about the cost of having a strong viewpoint, or a viewpoint that differs from that of others.

Waiting

But it is for you, O LORD, that I wait;
it is you, O LORD my God, who will answer.
(Psalm 38:15)

"Mom, can we go now?" asked the nine-year-old as she cornered her mother by the refrigerator. "All the kids have gone and there's nothing to do."

"We can go in fifteen to twenty minutes," the mother replied. "There are some things I need to talk to your aunt about. Why don't you go outside and play?"

"But there's nothing to do—we've already been playing. When can we go?"

It's hard for kids to wait, especially when it seems as if there's nothing to do. Nothing happens quickly enough. The time never goes fast enough. Answers never come soon enough. It's just wait, wait, wait.

Come to think of it, it's hard to wait as adults too. Forget about the few minutes in the grocery store checkout line or waiting for the pickles to be placed on your hamburger or even waiting for the construction traffic congestion to clear while driving in the car. That's kid stuff. How about times you're waiting for God when serious life issues are surrounding you, times when you wonder where in the world God is? How about times during a major life transition, times during an extended illness or the death of a loved one or strained relationships with your spouse or friend?

How about times when you're not at fault, when the problem is not of your own making, when suddenly out of nowhere, life throws you a curve ball? Or how about times when you've been patient and trusting in God's intervention, when you've done everything you're supposed to do and more, and yet nothing seems to happen? "God, can we move on now?" is one of the questions that may come to mind. "When can we leave that other stuff behind and get on to the good stuff? When can my life have real meaning? When will things get back to normal? When am I going to see the other side of the mountain?"

While it may appear a little too obvious at first, it's worth noting

111

anyway. When you're waiting for answers to your questions, it is important to ask the right person. It is important to ask the person who can do something about the situation. The nine-year-old girl in the example above did not ask her neighbor or cousin or dog or sister when she could leave. She asked her mother because she knew from experience that her mother was the one who could make the decision to leave. Her mother was going home to the same place she was. Her mother had the car keys. Her mother was the one who cared for her and had the daughter's personal best interests in mind.

The same thing is true when we are waiting for God. It is important to ask the right person. It is important to ask God since God has our personal well-being in mind. It is God who cares for us, loves us, and nurtures us. It is God who gives us our daily bread. It is God who is able to fulfill our daily needs. And yet, how often do we look elsewhere for our questions when we are waiting for God? If the answer isn't immediate, the temptation is to try something else—another job, another relationship, another "something."

"It is for you, O LORD, that I wait," writes the psalmist. "It is you, O LORD my God, who will answer." May our asking and waiting and trusting and hoping lie in God's hands.

To make this devotion your own:

- Tell about a time you waited and waited. What made it difficult to wait? If you were impatient, did it speed things up?
- In terms of your faith, do you think you are a patient person? Why or why not?
- Think of ways you can, or you have, waited patiently for God to answer your prayer.

Wilderness

But the people were thirsty and kept on complaining, "Moses, did you bring us out of Egypt just to let us and our families and our animals die of thirst?"

(Exodus 17:3 CEV)

There is nothing gradual about the terrain in the Judean wilderness. You know at once that the steep hills forced themselves up through the earth's surface like a taut, flexed muscle. Shoulders of steep limestone pop up from the plain without warning. The contrasts are striking. As you look across this vast wilderness off into the distance, limestone walls surround you in every direction as though you are inside a huge box. A few tufts of grass and shrub dot the landscape, but otherwise there is little vegetation. The first thought that comes to mind is this: How can anything survive out here?

This is the land where Jesus walked. But it is also the land where the children of Israel walked almost two thousand years before Jesus. It is no surprise that the Israelites, who came from the lush green delta plains of Egypt, suddenly wondered if Moses had taken a wrong turn. Food and water had never even been an issue before. Never had they given it a second thought. Whereas before the mood of the pharaoh had determined their living conditions, now they were at the mercy of this unforgiving wilderness. Now they did not worry about the quality of living—they wondered about life itself and how long they could survive without food and water. This harsh, barren land did not give up or yield anything easily.

In many respects, we are still in the wilderness like the children of Israel. While we may feel safe and secure and pampered one minute, the next minute may find us feeling helpless, alone, and vulnerable. A fight with a spouse, a job change, a sudden illness, or unexpected expenses may suddenly make us feel as if our green world has changed into a barren wilderness. Or temptation will remind us that we do not always have the things of God in mind. Sin in the world will always surround us and box us in like the Judean wilderness.

We know, however, that we do not need to stay in the wilderness

113

fighting for our survival by ourselves. Even as God provided food and water for the Israelites to save them in the wilderness, so God provides for us the life-nourishing gifts of forgiveness from sins and everlasting life. God's life-giving Spirit is as close to us as a quick plea or cry for help. We are not alone, even if we have carved out a barren place for ourselves by our thoughts, actions, or attitudes.

Next time you find yourself in the wilderness, whether made by yourself or by circumstances that surround you, let God hear you. Don't hesitate to cry out to God. Let God know how you feel and what you need. God will provide. And though we may not always find our journeys easy, we will always find in God a willing companion who will never leave us nor forsake us.

To make this devotion your own:

• Recall a time when you felt like you were alone or in the wilderness.
• Is your first inclination to cry out to God or to remain silent when you find yourself in a trying situation? Why?
• Tell one way you refresh yourself spiritually.

Wobbles

Draw near to God, and he will draw near to you.
(James 4:8)

Michael, the neighbor's six-year-old boy, was learning to ride his bike without training wheels. His short practice runs were precarious at best as he struggled to keep his balance. "I need a new bike," he said to his dad after one of his short practice jaunts down the block.

Since the bike was just a few years old and still in good shape, the surprised father asked, "Why's that? I thought you liked your bike."

"Oh, I do," he said, "but I need to get one that doesn't wobble so much."

Sometimes our spiritual walk is like learning to get the wobbles out. In the early stages we think the bike is the problem, when really all we need to do is to get a little more balance. With a little more time, with a little more practice, with a little more patience and understanding, our slow "wobbles" begin to straighten out as we move our eyes from our front tires, to the road ahead, to God. The writer of the letter of James gives some sound advice for those who want to keep their travels in life steady. "Draw near to God," he says, "and he will draw near to you."

Draw near to God. This reminds us that we need to be intentional about our relationship with God. Like any other relationship we experience in life, if we want our relationship to grow with someone else, we need to invest time and energy into that relationship. Take a moment to think about a good relationship you have with a friend, a coworker, a neighbor, or spouse. Chances are you've invested both quantity and quality time into that relationship. It wasn't something that just happened—the relationship evolved over time. You've been able to work through the "wobbles"—the struggles, disagreements, or misunderstandings you've had along the way—because you've practiced and practiced. You know how to adjust, to compensate, to steer your way clear and to keep things in balance.

So it is with God. We do not learn all there is to know about God by spending a few minutes at church or in prayer. It takes time. It takes practice. It means being intentional about finding the time to be with God. And as we become more intentional, more focused in our pursuit of knowing God and drawing near to God, God will draw near to us.

There is one hitch, however, a sticky point that keeps us from this desired relationship with God. We pull away. We back off. We keep our distance because we've done something wrong. We've sinned, and we feel ashamed or guilty. We do not want to draw near to God. We don't want to get close. We've taken a few spills on the bike and let our fears keep us away from getting back to the one who before gave us so much joy.

What is the answer? Draw near to God. *We* need to take the step of drawing closer to God. *We* need to face our discomfort and fear. *We* need to be intentional about being with God so that our wobbles will eventually turn into balance. God has already forgiven us and is simply waiting for us to return. Draw near to God, and God will draw near to you.

To make this devotion your own:

• Tell about a time when you felt near to God.
• Tell about a time when you felt far away from God.
• What helps you draw near to God or stay focused on God?